The Glory of Kings

is to search out a matter

A DEVOTIONAL AID

Phil John

The Glory of Kings copyright © 2024 by Phil John.

All rights reserved. No part of this book may be reproduced in any form or by any electronic or mechanical means including information storage and retrieval systems, without permission in writing from the author. The only exception is by a reviewer, who may quote short excerpts in a review.

Scripture quotations, unless otherwise indicated, are taken from The Holy Bible,
New International Version® (Anglicised), NIV®
Copyright © 1979, 1984, 2011 by Biblica, Inc.
Used by permission of Biblica, Inc. ® All rights reserved worldwide.

Scripture quotations marked (NLT) are taken from the *Holy Bible*, New Living Translation, copyright ©1996, 2004, 2015 by Tyndale House Foundation. Used by permission of Tyndale House Publishers, Carol Stream, Illinois 60188. All rights reserved.

Scripture quotations marked MSG are taken from *The Message*, copyright © 1993, 2002, 2018 by Eugene H. Peterson. Used by permission of NavPress. All rights reserved. Represented by Tyndale House Publishers.

Scripture quotations are from the ESV® Bible (The Holy Bible, English Standard Version®), © 2001 by Crossway, a publishing ministry of Good News Publishers. Used by permission. All rights reserved.

Revised Standard Version of the Bible, copyright 1952 [2nd edition, 1971] by the Division of Christian Education of the National Council of the Churches of Christ in the United States of America. Used by permission. All rights reserved.

Scripture quotations taken from the Amplified® Bible (AMPC), Copyright © 1954, 1958, 1962, 1964, 1965, 1987 by The Lockman Foundation Used by permission.

All emphases in Scripture quotations have been added by the author.

Cover design by the author, based on a suggestion from Paul Manwaring and graphically enhanced by Tom Hind. Typesetting by the author.

SPECIAL SALES

UK based organisations, churches, pastors and small group leaders can receive special discounts when purchasing this book.
For more information, please send an email to phil.john@thegloryofkings.co.uk

ENDORSEMENTS

It is my joy to call Phil John a true friend. I've watched his walk and pursuit of God for many years and his hunger, passion and integrity are an inspiration.

I was so blessed when Phil told me he had written a devotional book, in fact if memory serves me correctly what he actually said was, "I've written a little devotional book". Talk about an understatement! What you hold in your hands is much more than devotional work. What you hold in your hand is a spiritual armoury that will inspire, inform and equip you for effective Christian ministry and life.

You will be drawn into deeper intimacy with God and you will be provoked and challenged in your character, faith and expectations.

This book is like no other devotion I have read, it gives much more than inspiration and comfort. It literally will ignite your faith and passion to press for more of God.

This book has a deep prophetic flow as well as sound foundational biblical truth. It is definitely not a book to read once or even in one go. I encourage you to read it slowly, allow God to work in your heart and keep it to hand to reach back to.

This is not a one-off book. It will become an anchor point for your walk with God and a tool to help others on this wonderful walk we have with God!

Dr Simon Braker
Co-Director of Legacy Ministries International

The Glory of Kings is a devotional book for the brave and for the treasure seeker. It is for those who are hungry enough for the Word of God to not just read the Bible but to let the Bible read them.

Phil has done some of the work for us, with an enticing array of topics and methods to seek God daily, but he has left the response up to us.

This is not so much a three-course meal as a 'tasting menu', and it does need to be tasted and sampled to reap its benefits. On the table are many different ways to connect with the God who loves us. There really is something for everyone... words to drink in and receive, study and discoveries to make for ourselves, poetry and romance, science and amazing facts, and so much more.

Why not dive in, and devour a rich diet of spiritual food that will bring joy to your journey with Jesus?

Susan Hind,
Senior Pastor, One Church Leicester

ACKNOWLEDGEMENTS

Decades ago, a dear friend told me I should write. My heart resonated with the thought, but I tucked the dream away in the back of my mind. There it remained on the shelf for many decades.

On the return journey from a ministry trip to Sweden Simon Braker, my friend, prophet and teacher told me that God had spoken to him earlier that day, indicating that I should write a devotional book. I was very excited on the one hand as it was a long-held dream to write - and confused on the other hand – as I had never imagined authoring this genre of book!

But as the weeks and months followed, and as I began to write, I became deeply aware that this option was better than any I had ever contemplated. I have learned so much through the process of studying and writing!

This book adopts a different approach to some other devotional aids, and in so doing my prayer is that you expand your understanding of God, that you dig deeper into His Word and that you allow Holy Spirit to take you from one degree of glory to another.

I want to convey my heartfelt gratitude to several others:

- to my wonderful daughter Joanna, for putting up with an absent father whilst I wrote,
- to Laurence, Hazel and Lois for their constant encouragement to keep going when I doubted myself,
- to Colin, Claire, Lois and Tom for giving a considerable amount of their time to review the text, their wisdom in checking its Biblical accuracy and their gentleness in recommending improvements.

I also want to pay tribute to every person who has nurtured my faith and walk with the Lord throughout my life! There are many of you and you know who you are!

"Praise be to the God and Father of our Lord Jesus Christ, who has blessed us in the heavenly realms with every spiritual blessing in Christ."

Ephesians 1:3

DEDICATION

And finally, I dedicate this book to the memory of my amazing wife who taught me three things which have become treasured legacies: the vitality of a life walking with the Holy Spirit, that it is possible to hear God speaking to me directly in prayer, and the huge benefits of keeping a journal. This book stems from these beautiful gifts that Katie lived, inspired and nurtured in me.

CONTENTS

FROM ME TO YOU	**1**		
Before You Begin	4		
Meditation	5		
Devotion	7		
Keeping A Journal	10		
Tools For Digging Deeper	14		
RESTORED	**15**	**WORSHIP**	**91**
To My Beautiful Daughters	17	Worship And Surrender	93
To My Noble Sons	20	Worship	97
Healing	23	Remember	100
Broken	26	Idols	105
Broken And Restored	31	Majesty	107
Renamed, Recommissioned	35	A Crescendo Of Worship	112
Strength And Power	40	Victory Amplified	114
WONDER	**43**	**WISDOM**	**117**
Chosen And Unique	45	The Key	119
It's Ridiculous	48	Wisdom	121
Tapestry	52	Do You?	124
Numbers	57	What…	126
Time	60	Unanswered Prayer	128
Logos	63	Seek First His Kingdom	130
Rhema	65	Stewardship	135
THE CROSS	**67**	**FEAR**	**139**
Freedom	69	Victory Means Victory	141
The Staging Of Salvation	72	Fear	143
Fragrance	75	Fear Of The Lord	147
39 Lashes Of Love	78	Fear Without God	149
What Am I?	82	Fear Not	152
Remembrance	84	True Fear Of The Lord	156
Inheritance	87	Mystery	159

THE HEART	**163**	**RELATIONSHIPS**	**199**
Choose Well	165	Be To Them As I Am	201
Always Or Sometimes	167	One Another	203
Pray For Your Heart	169	All Or Some	205
My Heart's State	170	Personalize	207
A Prayer For Your Heart	171	Never	210
Pray This For Your Heart	172	For Ever And Ever	212
My Heart's Response	174	Keep In The Blessing	214
HOLY SPIRIT	**177**	**GLORY**	**219**
Equipped For Victory	179	Glory Manifest	221
Alongside	181	Glory Of The Lord	224
Paraklesis	185	Jesus' Glory	225
Watermark	188	The Nature Of Glory	226
Thirsty	191	What His Glory Looks Like	228
Refreshment	194	In Light Of His Glory	229
Waymaker	196	The Glory Of Kings	231
		EPILOGUE	**233**

FROM ME TO YOU

I named this book from the verse below:

> *'It is the glory of God to conceal a matter;*
> *to search out a matter is the glory of kings'*
> Proverbs 25:2

It's a tricky text!

My take-out from the first half is that God reveals everything that we need, but in His infinite wisdom keeps some things hidden. It's His choice and who are we to argue? According to Isaiah 55:9 'As the heavens are higher than the earth, so are my ways higher than your ways and my thoughts than your thoughts.'

However, the second half of the verse intimates that there is an opportunity for us to explore God's character and dig deeper into His Word in order that we can better understand Him. In order to do this, we unequivocally need Holy Spirit's help to 'search out a matter!'

2 Corinthians 3:18 reminds us that this is a continual process of going deeper enabled by Holy Spirit.

'And we all, who with unveiled faces contemplate the Lord's glory, are being transformed into his image with ever-increasing glory, which comes from the Lord, who is the Spirit.'

My intent for the pages that follow is to provide a guide, a signpost, a stimulus, a provocation to thought. The value will be in what Holy Spirit reveals to you as you prayerfully consider each topic, each question and 'search out a matter'.

That will be the lasting treasure. The more you reflect with Holy Spirit, the more that you will uncover what God is saying to you.

I have intentionally not given you the whole answer on anything (not that I have it in any case!) but rather attempted to awaken new thoughts in you and invite you to go deeper and to figure things out for yourself as you 'search out each matter'. Convictions cannot be handed to you. I cannot make you learn. If, at any time, you are moved to repentance, praise, thanksgiving, worship, understanding, action, change or surrender – then I can consider time spent in laying down these thoughts as valuable.

> *'Whatever exists is far off and most profound—*
> *who can discover it?*
> *So I turned my mind to understand,*
> *to investigate and to search out wisdom and the scheme of things*
> *and to understand the stupidity of wickedness*
> *and the madness of folly.'*

Ecclesiastes 7:24-25

I have attempted to illustrate a variety of different ways of looking at things making use of personal testimony, word studies, examination of the original Hebrew and Greek, in depth Bible studies, prophetic words, meditations, a look at numbers, personalised scripture, questions, names, parallel pictures of Biblical themes, paraphrases, prayers and more. No one exploration approach is better than another and not all may suit you, but I encourage you to experiment as you work through this book and get to know our amazing God even better.

Consider the Word of God as a multi-faceted diamond. It is one entity but as you view it from different angles you see different colours and light. Whatever your circumstance or perspective there is always something new to glimpse and discover.

There are 70 'devotions' to aid you on your journey. Whether you take minutes, hours, or even days on each is up to you, but don't be in a hurry! Each devotion is followed by the invitation to:

'Now Search Out The Matter'

in line with the title and objective of this book. These include questions, suggestions and ideas for going deeper. Prepare to push back the boundaries of your understanding, go deeper and discover new things!

> This book is for:
> treasure hunters,
> gold prospectors,
> truth archaeologists,
> glory explorers,
> adventure seekers
> and wisdom detectives
> willing to investigate with Holy Spirit!
>
> If that's you, then read on…

BEFORE YOU BEGIN

Before you dive in, I'd like to review four topics with you by way of preparation for what follows: meditation, devotion, keeping a journal and some tools for digging deeper.

Please **don't** do what I often do, which is to speed-read the introduction so I can get to the meat faster! I want to help you frame your approach to going deeper.

MEDITATION

In my twenties, I was taught that meditation could be likened to rumination - chewing the cud. This is a process where a cow repeatedly regurgitates grass or feed and chews it again. A cow has four parts to its stomach to conduct this process - swallowing is not enough so repeated chewing is required. It was a very helpful picture for me in explaining how I needed to approach God's Word – value comes from reading it – greater value comes from chewing it over!

There are many ways to look at meditation. Here are some definitions.

To meditate is to consider thoughtfully, to study, to engage in contemplation, to consider deeply, to muse, to ruminate, to cogitate, to reflect upon, to turn over in the mind, to intend, to exercise the mind.

Meditation is sustained reflection, a devotional exercise, thoughtfulness, lateral thinking, pondering, deeply thinking through and focusing on a subject.

Each description above requires intent, time, effort, and a willingness to learn and change. The Biblical principle, 'you reap what you sow' applies here (see Galatians 6:7-9). The more we invest in seeking God, the greater the return from Him.

The word meditate appears 21 times in the Old Testament, of which 19 are in the Psalms. In Joshua 1:8, Joshua is told:

'Keep this Book of the Law always on your lips; meditate on it day and night, so that you may be careful to do everything written in it. Then you will be prosperous and successful.'

This is echoed in Psalm 1:1-2, where blessing is associated with one whose 'delight is in the law of the Lord, and who meditates on his law day and night'. In Psalm 19:14 the Psalmist prays 'may these words of my mouth and this meditation of my heart be pleasing in your sight'. Elsewhere in the Psalms we see the writer meditates on 'His wonderful and mighty deeds', 'His decrees' and 'His unfailing love' - a comprehensive list of what we are to reflect upon!

Meditating on God's Word is crucial to our understanding of who He is, who we were, who we now are and who we will become. Meditation is a gateway to prosperity, success, delight and pleasing the Lord. The Bible clearly points us to meditation of the Truth. This works for me, and I highly recommend it to you!

I have presented a range of material for you to chew on. I have intentionally varied the style of presentation to aid you in broadening your approach to meditation. I now hand this over for you to contemplate! Pray as the Psalmist did before you read further:

'May these words of my mouth and this meditation of my heart be pleasing in your sight, Lord, my Rock and my Redeemer.'
                                                              Psalm 19:14

DEVOTION

David, a man after God's heart, makes a public appeal to his son Solomon in the sight of all Israel:

> 'And you, my son Solomon, acknowledge the God of your father, and serve him with wholehearted devotion and with a willing mind, for the LORD searches every heart and understands every desire and every thought. If you seek him, he will be found by you; but if you forsake him, he will reject you for ever.'
> 1 Chronicles 28:9

Ezra 'devoted himself to the study and observance of the law of the Lord, and to teaching its decrees and laws in Israel' (Ezra 7:10)

Nehemiah devoted himself to rebuilding the wall surrounding Jerusalem. His devotion led to the restoration of the wall which was completed in just 52 days!

The early church, in Acts 2:42, 'devoted themselves to the apostles' teaching and to fellowship, to the breaking of bread and to prayer.'

Paul urges the Colossians in chapter 4 verse 2: 'Devote yourselves to prayer, being watchful and thankful'.

Paul devoted himself 'exclusively to preaching, testifying to the Jews that Jesus was the Messiah' (Acts 18:5), and in Romans 12:10 Paul calls us to 'be devoted to one another in love'. Elsewhere in Paul's letters we are called to devote ourselves to prayer; to being watchful and thankful; and to all kinds of good deeds. Challenging eh!

When I was dating the woman who would become my wife, I was utterly devoted to spending every moment that I could with her; to thinking about her; to writing and hiding special love messages around her house, or under the windscreen wipers of her car; to buying her gifts. My thoughts were consumed with her. I would do anything for her. I just wanted to be with her. I was devoted to her – only her.

God expects us to devote ourselves to our family, friends, relationships and work for His glory. However, our primary devotion must be to God and His Kingdom. 1 Corinthians 7:29-31 implores us as follows:

'What I mean, brothers and sisters, is that the time is short. From now on those who have wives should live as if they do not; those who mourn, as if they did not; those who are happy, as if they were not; those who buy something, as if it were not theirs to keep; those who use the things of the world, as if not engrossed in them. For this world in its present form is passing away.'

Is your first love for God as it once was? Does it need rekindling? (Revelation 2:4 and Jeremiah 2:2)

Devotion demands commitment and a singular focus. It springs out of love and is all-consuming. It costs.

I'll leave you with the Lord's question (Jeremiah 30:21)

> 'Who is he who will devote himself
> to be close to me?'

Will you?

THE GLORY OF KINGS

As I wrote the above, I sensed God saying to me:

My child,

Will you devote yourself wholly to me?
Will you love me without question?
Will you prioritize me above all else?

Do you thirst for me?
Do you long for our next encounter?
Do you want nothing but me?

Have you yielded every plan?
Have you surrendered every thought?
Have you laid down your life for me?

How much was my sacrifice worth?
How much is my love for you?
How much do you think of me?

Will you go where I send you?
Will you do what I ask of you?
Will you serve me whatever the cost?

I was devoted to you from the first moment I created you.
I am devoted to you each and every day.
I am devoted to transforming you to be like my Son.

I made you; I blessed you; I sacrificed my Son for you,
I forgave you; I washed you clean; I made you new,
I gave you eternal life, I pour out my love on you daily,

Is it too much for me to ask for
your wholehearted devotion?

KEEPING A JOURNAL

My wife was a notebook fan. They were many in number and various in their coloured and patterned covers, but typically had lined pages and were spiral bound. In fact, she acquired and used many notebooks, and she had the habit of leaving them either hidden or exposed all around the house! She really could have done with a further notebook to log all the others, their dates and their locations! She used them for two primary purposes. One was to record vital information like notes from her medical consultations, key phone numbers, and so on. The second, and by far the biggest consumer of these notebooks, were journals of her conversations with God, recorded during the precious time that she spent in true devotion with Him and listening to His voice.

Sometimes, these would record a brief question to her Father, followed by longer replies as she listened and captured what God was saying to her. Sometimes there were no questions, she simply recorded what God was saying to her. On some occasions she would hear Him speak in English. At other times, she would pray in tongues and then capture the interpretation as the Holy Spirit enabled her.

As a young child, the school nurse would visit her parents, concerned that she wasn't getting enough sleep, often implying that her parents must be doing something to cause this problem! Truth be told, sleep was something that frequently evaded her throughout the 38 years we were together. Having been misdiagnosed for a decade, we eventually learned that the true diagnosis was that of a very rare type of cancer. It was a further seven years before she was invited home to be with Jesus – seven years in which the cancer spread, caused increasing pain and where her sleep was disrupted even further. Despite spending many nights awake, she chose to pray, to listen to God, to learn more about the Holy Spirit and His gifts, to watch material online to advance her spiritual understanding, to read the Bible, to read books, to take notes of her learning, and to journal her conversations with God.

She used her time in the day to pursue these activities too. Some days, she'd even ask me if I'd like to go for a walk, or a drive, so that she could grab a couple of uninterrupted hours with God, with me out of the way! These times were her lifeline, yielding more value than any other pursuit. The cancer and pain in her body were **never** an excuse for her not to pursue God.

I was staggered at how her walk with God developed during the hardest years of her life. Her times with Him were the source of her strength, and her journal of their conversations provided her with such encouragement as she re-read the entries at later dates.

She taught me three things in those seven years that formed treasured legacies for me. Firstly, the vitality of a life walking with the Holy Spirit. Secondly, that it was possible to hear God speaking to me directly in prayer (I only knew how to hear through His Word, and by the occasional gentle nudge to act). Thirdly, and by example, the huge benefits in keeping a journal.

I started on a journey to hear God, just as Katie did, creating my first journal in January 2019, with a daily record of one or more questions to God, and writing down His response. After several years, I stopped asking questions every single day, and simply initiated that day's conversation, with these two words – 'Just listening' – and then waiting to see what He wanted to say to me.

I had no idea, when I started, just how important and how valuable this record would be. I had a great memory when I was young, but like many of my peers, it's become poorer as I have aged! I have been so encouraged each time I go back to review a few months of my journal. Things which I captured earlier, were there to reflect and meditate upon. There are times when I've been more amazed and blessed in retrospect than on the day when I recorded what God said! It is likely that I didn't take time to really let His words sink in or impact me at the moment of their receipt.

I could wax lyrical about this, but nothing will replace or trump your own experiences. Some of you are smiling at me now, as you've been doing this a lot longer, and are glad I got there at last!! Some of you have never journaled.

For the latter, I thought a few practical hints might be helpful:

- Always set aside time to be with Him
- A short conversation with Him is better than no conversation!
- Catch what God says there and then – don't delay!
- Write exactly what you hear, even if it doesn't make sense at the time
- Capture the date of each entry
- Make space to meditate upon and pray about what He speaks to you during this time
- Don't be too ambitious at the start
- Don't beat yourself up if you miss a day!
- There's nothing that you cannot ask God
- There's no emotion that you cannot express to Him
- Review your journal, every week or every month or every year (for that week, or that month, or that year)
- Make sure you have taken steps to obey – if you didn't at the time, it's never too late – act now!
- My wife's preference was to use pen and paper, recording everything in notebooks. I prefer a digital approach…

- I started by typing into a Notes App on my phone; then I switched to using Gboard within the Notes App (as I'm not a proficient typist!!)
- I would then email these notes to myself so that I could capture them in a Word Document on my laptop (with the advantage that I can back up my journal regularly – it's too valuable to lose!)
- More recently I started to use a (voice) Recorder App on my phone, which captures an audio copy as I speak what I hear; the App then allows me to transcribe what I have spoken into text, which can then be added to the digital copy of the journal
- Each to their own! Choose what suits you best!

Everyone is different - there is no right way of doing this! It's up to you as to what you record: it may just be what God says to you that day, and/or a scripture and your thoughts, a dream, a vision or a picture; notes from a message at church, or from an online video or podcast. It could be a special event that occurred on the day which God used to speak to you, or a conversation with a friend, or how God blessed you. The choice is yours! This is for you, no-one else!!!

TOOLS FOR DIGGING DEEPER

The following tool list is far from exhaustive – it's a place to start if you haven't already! They are free and online, and often with Apps for your mobile phone.

- YouVersion Bible App
  (https://www.youversion.com/the-bible-app/)

- BibleGateway
  (https://www.biblegateway.com/)

- Bible Hub App
  (https://biblehub.com/)

- Bible Project
  (https://bibleproject.com/)

- Blue Letter Bible
  (https://www.blueletterbible.org/)

- eSword
  (https://www.e-sword.net/)

RESTORED

- ❖ To My Beautiful Daughters
- ❖ To My Noble Sons
- ❖ Healing
- ❖ Broken
- ❖ Broken And Restored
- ❖ Renamed And Recommissioned
- ❖ Strength And Power

*'Your identity is not found in
what you do,
or don't do,
or what happens to you.
It is found in Christ Jesus.'*

Lisa Osteen Comes

TO MY BEAUTIFUL DAUGHTERS

Come and sit with me.
Sit at my feet and let me speak into your heart.

I see in you a beauty that no other sees.
I have made you more beautiful than anything that your eyes perceive.
I have made you to stand glorious in my presence.
There is nothing about you that I do not love.

I have made you to be unique.
There is none like you.
In amongst millions and billions I recognize you as an individual upon whom my love is pouring.

I speak to those lies inside of you that say others consider you to be plain or uninteresting or mistaken or foolish.

I only see the developing heart of my Son in your life.
You carry who I AM.
You carry the beauty of my holiness, and I have made you righteous and clean.
There is nothing in you that I do not love.

I love to be with you.
I long to spend even more time with you.

Don't believe everything that you hear said about you.
Consider only the words that I have spoken to you.
Consider what I'm saying to you now, for my love goes deeper and further.
My love covers a multitude of sins.
So, stand up my daughters -
In the grace which I have poured on you.
Listen only to my voice.

THE GLORY OF KINGS

Seek only the holiness that comes from me.
Pursue the beauty that only I can bestow through my Spirit.

I am changing you from one degree of glory to another.
Do not resist my gentle hand.
Defend yourself against the words of the enemy by eating my words – your daily bread!
Spend time in my presence and not in his.

I see all the brokenness,
and the tears,
and the pain,
The words which have hurt,
and the thoughts which have led you astray.
Renew your mind now as you sit with me.
Gaze into my eyes and see the love that I have for you.

Nothing is more special for me,
than to have you sit with me right now,
to have you walk with me.
Being with you thrills my heart.
I take great delight in you.
Nothing can separate you from my love.
I long for the next time that we will meet.
I wait with excitement in anticipation of the next walk that we will take together.

I only think about pouring goodness into you.
I want to bestow all my riches upon you,
as you stand radiant in my glory.
My daughters - go out in strength!
Be certain of who you are because of your standing in me!

What others see will pass away.
What I see,
and what I build in you,
will endure forever.

You are so blessed.
You are so, so blessed.

I love you.

The Father

Now Search Out the Matter

---

1. Ask to see yourself as He sees you. Sometimes how we view ourselves is different from how God sees us. How does your view need to change?

2. Read and meditate on the following passages as interpreted in The Passion Translation of the Bible and refresh your understanding of the depth of His love for you in Song of Songs 1:8-11 and 5:1; and your response to His love in Song of Songs 5:10-16. Check out other Bible versions too.

Note: Whilst this is a corporate word for women, I call on every man who reads this to make a special time for prayer today, to bring all the beautiful women in their lives before God. There are plenty of themes within the above to inform your thanksgiving and intercession on their behalf!

TO MY NOBLE SONS

My sons, come and sit with me at the city gate.
Take time out from your busy schedule,
and rest a while with me.
I have important things to discuss with you,
but these will require your full attention.
Set aside everyday matters which consume you.
Relinquish the distractions which fill your time.
Pass your burdens to me and
let go of them completely.
Rest in my presence.
No words.
No requests.
Just relax and listen.
My sheep hear my voice- when they are still!

Who are you?
Are you having an identity crisis?
What defines you?
Why is it that you seek the honour that men afford?
Don't let the opinions of others shape you.
The praise of men is finite and shallow.
You are my handiwork, formed perfectly for your destiny.
Why do you strive for position, recognition and glory?
Why try to earn what I have already made available to you?
Have you forgotten your inheritance?

My estimation of you is eternal.
It's independent of what you've achieved.
It doesn't focus on failure.
It was redeemed at the highest price.
It releases you to be who I created you to be.
You are loved, chosen and forgiven.
You are a prince of the Most High.
A child of the King of Kings.

THE GLORY OF KINGS

A noble of the highest order.
A royal priest.

Use the abilities I have given you for others.
Use the gifts I have given you for my body, my kingdom.
Use your time wisely, it's my gift to you.
I've provided time for all that you need to do.
Most of all - take time to be with me.

All authority in heaven and on earth is mine.
Now wield the authority I have given you!
To raise the dead to life again.
To drive out demons.
To cure diseases.
To trample on snakes.
To overcome all the power of the enemy!
...yes ALL!

Be strong in me, your Lord, and in my mighty power!
You received power when my Holy Spirit came upon you.
Be my witnesses.
My noble sons, it is time to robe yourselves in truth,
to put on the whole armour of God,
to be bold and courageous,
mighty men of valour.
Stay very close,
keep your eyes on me,
listen carefully to my still small voice.

I love you,
The Father

Now Search Out the Matter
---

1. Ask to see yourself as He sees you. Sometimes how we view ourselves is different from how God sees us. How does your view need to change?

2. Read and meditate on the following passages: 1 Peter 2:5-10 (especially v9); Ephesians 6:10-20; Colossians 2:6-10 (especially v8); Romans 12:1-2; Psalm 139.

Note: Whilst this is a corporate word for men, I call on every woman who reads this to make a special time for prayer today, to bring all the noble men in their lives before God. There are plenty of themes within the above to inform your thanksgiving and intercession on their behalf!

HEALING

Jesus provides us with the best example when it comes to healing. Whilst he could have used his divine power to complete all His tasks on earth, Jesus always chose to live as a human being accessing His relationship with the Father and empowered by the Spirit.

We cannot say, 'It was different for Jesus because He is God, and we are not; or that He could do things which we are unable to do because He is God.' Philippians 2:5-7 tells us:

'Have the same mindset as Christ Jesus: who, being in very nature God, did not consider equality with God something to be used to his own advantage; rather, he made himself nothing by taking the very nature of a servant, being made in human likeness.'

Jesus provides the perfect illustration of how we are to live, and the possibilities available to us if we live in relationship with the Father empowered by the Spirit.

Jesus only did what He saw His Father doing. He could do nothing by Himself (John 5:19):

'Jesus gave them this answer: 'Very truly I tell you, the Son can do nothing by himself; he can do only what he sees his Father doing, because whatever the Father does the Son also does."

Furthermore, Jesus only said what He heard the Father saying. In John 12:49-50 we read:

'For I did not speak on my own, but the Father who sent me commanded me to say all that I have spoken. I know that his command leads to eternal life. So whatever I say is just what the Father has told me to say.'

In the New Testament there are 20 recorded occasions of Jesus' words when He healed, restored or delivered.

I discovered some crucial facts:

Jesus uses as few as 1 word, and a maximum of 17!

(I've counted the English words translated from the Greek, but if you wish you can check the number used in Greek - and you will find the same brevity!)

Jesus always commanded with authority:

"Rise and go! "
"Be clean!"
"Be opened!"
"Go in peace and be freed!"
"Come out!"
"Get up!"
"Go wash!"

Jesus always rewarded faith:

"Your faith has made you well."
"Let it be done just as you believed it would!"
"Your faith has healed you!"
"According to your faith, let it be done to you."
"For such a reply you may go – the demon has left your daughter."

Jesus often started out with a question:

"Who touched my clothes?"
"Shall I come and heal him?"
"What is your name?"
"Do you want to get well?"
"Which is easier to say, 'your sins are forgiven' or to say 'get up and walk'"
"What do you want me to do for you?"
"Do you believe I am able to do this?"

"Why all this commotion and wailing?"

Jesus healed everyone who *came* to Him seeking to be well.

Conversely, Jesus did not heal everyone who was sick – in John 5 we only see Jesus healing the paralytic man – not the 'great number' who used to lie by the pool.

Now Search Out the Matter
---

1. Check out healing accounts found in the following chapters for yourself:

    - Matthew 4, 8, 9, 12, 15, 17
    - Mark 1, 2, 3, 5, 7, 9, 10
    - Luke 4, 5, 6, 7, 8, 9, 13, 17, 18

2. Apply Jesus' short prayer principle the next time you pray for someone's healing. It's our faith that counts, not the length of our prayers!

3. If you don't see results immediately use the principles in the following verses: Luke 11:9, Matthew 7:9-11

4. Read the following verses: Matthew 14:23; Mark 6:46; Luke 6:12, Mark 1:35; Luke 5:16; John 12:49-50. Do you think that there is any connection between how Jesus spent His time and His ability to heal?

BROKEN

Most of us know that it's possible to be broken by circumstances, by external factors, but is it conceivable that we could be broken by God? I can already hear some of you reacting angrily at the thought. It sounds theologically unsound and at best emotionally unacceptable! Nevertheless, I believe God is willing to break us - and does - when it's for our good. This may be necessary when we become rebellious, too proud or too independent. His heart is always for our best – always.

He never crushes us completely, though that will be the fate of those who stubbornly refuse to acknowledge Him as their Lord. Jesus makes this very clear in Luke 20:17-18:

Jesus looked directly at them and asked, "Then what is the meaning of that which is written:

> 'The stone the builders rejected
> has become the cornerstone?'
> Everyone who falls on that stone will be broken to pieces; anyone on whom it falls will be crushed."

But will God break those of us who do acknowledge his Lordship? The story of Jacob provides a clue. Having wrestled all night with an angel of God, Jacob comes through as a changed person, and is left with a limp for the rest of his life - as a reminder.

> 'Then the man said, 'Your name will no longer be Jacob, but Israel, because you have struggled with God and with humans and have overcome."
> Genesis 32:28

From the point of this encounter, Israel (Jacob) was never the same again.

As a child I learned many choruses at Sunday School - one that I loved, and still love, is:

> 'Spirit of the Living God,
> Fall afresh on me,
> Spirit of the Living God,
> Fall afresh on me,
> Break me, melt me, mould me, fill me.
> Spirit of the Living God,
> Fall afresh on me.'
>
> Daniel Iverson, 1926

I noticed a few years back that a newer version had appeared where the line,

> 'Break me, melt me, mould me, fill me'

had been replaced by…

> 'Melt me, mould me, fill me, use me.'

In making this change the phrase 'Break me' has been removed, seemingly softening the original language – though I'm not sure that being 'melted' by the fire of God is any less uncomfortable!

Would a loving God break us? I am convinced, that if we need to be broken to be transformed into the likeness of Jesus by Holy Spirit as we surrender to Him, God's love will not stop short of doing what is necessary.

Let's look at it another way. What other words are ascribed to God's actions that we might not feel emotionally comfortable with?

God 'tests' us as he did Abraham (check out Genesis 22:1). The Hebrew word here, nasah (נָסָה), means to test or try. The same word is used in Exodus 16:4 where God tests His people. This is different from being tempted – see James 1:13-14. James 1:2-4 calls us to:

'Consider it pure joy, my brothers and sisters, whenever you face trials of many kinds, because you know that the testing of your faith produces perseverance. Let perseverance finish its work so that you may be mature and complete, not lacking anything.'

God testing or trying our faith is Biblical, and it is for our benefit so that we may be complete.

Jesus, Himself, called us to take up our cross and follow Him (Matthew 16:24). Paul calls us to join with him in suffering for the Gospel (2 Timothy 1:8). As His disciples we will face trouble and persecution (Matthew 13:20-21); similarly in John 16:33 where we are told to expect 'trouble' or suffering, tribulation, persecution, and distress.

The Bible never teaches that life is going to be easy! In fact, the only reference I could find to the word 'easy' in Scripture was in Matthew 11:28:30, 'For my yoke is easy, and my burden is light.' God's Word is not always comfortable. If He is willing to test and try us, to allow us to walk through suffering and distress, then the thought that He would consider breaking us may not seem so distant.

Let me ask you this: do you baulk at the idea of a horse being 'broken in'? Does it ruin a horse's life? Once upon a time, 'breaking a horse' meant forcing the animal into obedience and crushing its wild spirit. Today, the process is much more refined. Any analogy can be stretched too far, but consider some similarities with how God 'breaks us in':

Breaking a horse in	Being broken by God
Is not easy to do	Is not easy to receive
Requires a gentle, patient and understanding trainer	Requires a gentle, merciful, patient and understanding Father
Continues until the horse is docile, calm, and submitted	Continues until we come to a place of repentance, peace and submission
Teaches the horse to trust	Teaches us to trust
Demands the horse to be obedient	Demands obedience to His divine will
Requires human contact as a priority	Requires our relationship with God to be the priority
Involves a bridle and a saddle	Involves an easy yoke and a light burden
Occurs in a safe and secure area	Occurs in His presence - in the shelter beneath His wings
Requires the horse to learn to stand still	Requires us to be still and know that He is God
Requires the horse to learn to walk	Requires us to step out in faith
Lasts until the horse knows who's master	Lasts until we fully know the Master

My testimony is one of being broken by God's love when I have been proud and arrogant, when I have wandered away from the path set before me, when I have acted in my own strength, when I have believed my plans were better than His as the suffering of a loved one seemed inexplicable.

I actively choose to pray 'Spirit of the Living God, fall afresh on me; break me, melt me, mould me, fill me.'

David's heart sacrifice to God was one of brokenness:

> 'My sacrifice, O God, is a broken spirit;
> a broken and contrite heart
> you, God, will not despise.'
> Psalm 51:17

Father, break the wild spirit in us. Lead us into obedience. And may we run free in the fields that you have prepared for us.

Now Search Out the Matter

---

1. Are you willing to be broken by His love?

2. Will you offer Him the sacrifice of your broken spirit? What does this look like for you today? What commitment will you make to Him?

3. Is there any time in your life that you recognize you stepped out of line with God's plan and followed your own path? How did God draw you back to Himself? How did this whole episode make you more like Jesus?

BROKEN AND RESTORED

A potter uses his hands and water to fashion a clay lump into a beautiful shape. The object is then ready to be decorated. After a glaze is added, it is fired at a high temperature to increase its strength.

God's children are hand crafted by the Almighty Potter, creating something beautiful and unique in every case.

'Yet you, Lord, are our Father. We are the clay, you are the potter; we are all the work of your hand.'

Isaiah 64:8

When the time was right, in Luke 4, Jesus initiated his ministry by reading from Isaiah in the synagogue in Nazareth. Let's look at the original passage:

'The Spirit of the Sovereign LORD is on me,
    because the LORD has anointed me
    to proclaim good news to the poor.
He has sent me to bind up the broken-hearted,
    to proclaim freedom for the captives
    and release from darkness for the prisoners,
to proclaim the year of the LORD's favour
    and the day of vengeance of our God,
to comfort all who mourn,
    and provide for those who grieve in Zion –
to bestow on them a crown of beauty
    instead of ashes,
the oil of joy
    instead of mourning,
and a garment of praise
    instead of a spirit of despair.
They will be called oaks of righteousness,

a planting of the LORD
   for the display of his splendour.'
Isaiah 61:1-3

Jesus declares Himself as the ultimate answer in Luke 4:21 "Today this scripture is fulfilled in your hearing."

The Greek word sózó (σῴζω) means salvation, healing and deliverance. We see all these elements in the Isaiah passage above. You will find them in Psalm 103:1-5 and Isaiah 53:1-6 as well - Saviour, Healer, and Deliverer.

Pots are easily cracked or broken – just as we are – however, that's what Jesus came to fix.

KINTSUGI

Kintsugi is the Japanese word for 'golden joinery'. Kintsukuroi, as it's also known, means 'golden repair'. It is an art form which deals in broken or cracked pottery. It uses gold, or gold dust in a lacquer, to cement together broken pieces of pottery, or to fill its cracks. It embraces what is cracked, broken, flawed and imperfect. It is a beautiful form of restoration. It reveals, rather than hides, the cracks, and the brokenness. The resulting objects are often worth more afterwards than they were before being damaged.

Our human decisions and experiences mean that we are all broken to some degree. We all need restoration. We need saving, healing, and delivering. Our brokenness often means we are badly damaged, unable to continue working properly. Brokenness can be caused by many things: illness (physical and mental), loss of a loved one, grief, anxiety, fear, corrupted identity, addiction, straying from God's path, unforgiveness, guilt, shame, poverty, abuse, the absence of love, and so on. It's not something we can repair on our own. Although we try to fix things, it is never lasting or complete. However, the good news is that we can be completely restored and set free!

Once restored, like a Kintsugi pot, the broken pieces are still evident, but bound together by bands of gold running through us, cementing us back to our original shape, our original design. These bands of golden restoration indicate our enormous value to our Creator. We see that we are, and are seen to be, highly treasured!

Paul sums it up well in 2 Corinthians 4:7-9

'But we have this treasure in jars of clay to show that this all-surpassing power is from God and not from us. We are hard pressed on every side, but not crushed; perplexed, but not in despair; persecuted, but not abandoned; struck down, but not destroyed.'

Once again, we see a reference to our frailty, like that of a clay pot. We also see that Paul is not crushed or abandoned.

I keep a Kintsugi teacup on my mantlepiece as a reminder that I was once utterly broken, as a symbol of my beautiful restoration as an object of thanksgiving for his grace and mercy and as a testimony to be shared with visitors who enquire as to its design or purpose.

Now Search Out the Matter

Have you been impacted by illness (physical or mental), loss of a loved one, grief, anxiety, fear, corrupted identity, addiction, poverty, abuse, or the absence of love? Have you allowed the Father to fully restore you? If you are still broken, then it's time to invite Him in to do what only He can do. This may take some time – God can fix you in an instant – but often there is a journey involved during which we can only cope with a bit at a time.

The following are some of the things you might consider engaging in by:

- obtaining a good grasp of what the Bible teaches about healing and restoration
- seeking prayer ministry
- achieving a better understanding of John 8:321-32: 'If you hold to my teaching, you are really my disciples. Then you will know the truth, and the truth will set you free.'
- reading some of the many books which address these issues

RENAMED AND RECOMISSIONED

In scripture we read about several significant people who are renamed following a life-changing *breakthrough* encounter with God. Breakthrough may be an important discovery or event that helps us to improve a situation or provide an answer to a problem, a sudden advance, an advance all the way through the enemy's front line, a sudden increase in knowledge or understanding and a significant progress achievement.

Biblically we could consider breakthrough as 'Heaven manifested on earth' resulting from having been in the presence of God or from living in the authority given to us because of the cross. Names, and the receipt of new names, are Biblically very significant breakthrough events. They represent an old identity being replaced by a new identity. Names are with you daily and as such unforgettable. God did not want these people to forget their new names. Nor does he want you to forget yours – but more of that when we have explored Bible characters who were renamed. Furthermore, these name changes were all prophetic, urging those concerned towards a new destiny.

Abram Is Renamed Abraham

Abraham was originally named Abram – meaning 'exalted father', but God changed his name to Abraham – meaning 'father of many, or of a multitude (see Genesis 17:3-6). The name change was significant as it indicated a new phase in Abraham's life and his relationship with God. God promised Abraham that he would be the father of many nations. Changing his name was a way of reaffirming that promise and emphasizing his role as the father of a great people – one of whom you are today!

Sarai Is Renamed Sarah

In the Old Testament, Sarah was originally named Sarai, but God changed her name to Sarah in Genesis 17:15-16. The name Sarai means 'my princess' while the name Sarah means 'princess' or 'noblewoman'. Sarah moves from being Abraham's (my) princess – she was a real beauty – to becoming a 'princess of many' alongside her husband as 'father of many'. As with Abraham, this signified a new phase of life, and relationship with God for Sarah. God promised Abraham that Sarah would give birth to a son, even though she was past the age of childbearing. Changing her name to Sarah was a way of emphasizing her role as the mother of the promised child and symbolizing her new identity as a woman of great importance in God's plan.

Jacob Is Renamed Israel
In the Old Testament, Jacob was renamed Israel by God. Jacob's original name means 'supplanter' or 'heel grabber', as he was born holding onto his twin brother Esau's heel. The name change occurred after Jacob wrestled with an angel of God throughout the night. During the struggle, the angel declared, 'Your name will no longer be Jacob, but Israel, because you have struggled with God and with humans and have overcome' (Genesis 32:28). The name Israel means 'he who struggles with God' or 'God contends'. This new name was significant because it represented a transformation in Jacob's character and identity. He was no longer just a heel-grabbing deceiver, but a man who had struggled with God and emerged victorious. From then on, he was known as Israel and became the father of the twelve tribes of Israel. As such he inherited the amazing promise given to his grandfather, Abraham.

Hoshea Is Renamed Joshua
In the Old Testament, Joshua was originally named Hoshea, which means 'salvation'. However, Moses renamed him Joshua in Numbers 13:16, which means 'Yahweh is salvation'. The renaming of Hoshea to Joshua occurred as Moses was preparing to send twelve spies to explore the land of Canaan. Moses changed Hoshea's name to Joshua as a way of

emphasizing his faith in God's ability to save and deliver His people. This name-change also indicated that Joshua would be a key figure in the conquest of Canaan and the fulfilment of God's promises to His people. From that day on, Joshua became a prominent person in Israel and eventually succeeded Moses as the leader of the Israelites. Under Joshua's leadership, the Israelites successfully conquered Canaan and established themselves in the land that God had promised them.

Simon Is Renamed Peter
In the New Testament, Simon was renamed Peter by Jesus. The name Simon means 'he has heard', while the name Peter means 'rock'. The renaming occurred in Matthew 16:17-18, where Jesus asked his disciples who they believed He was. Simon Peter responded, 'You are the Messiah, the Son of the living God.' In response, Jesus said, 'Blessed are you, Simon son of Jonah, for this was not revealed to you by flesh and blood, but by my Father in heaven. And I tell you that you are Peter, and on this rock, I will build my church, and the gates of Hades will not overcome it'. The name change from Simon to Peter symbolized the new role that Peter would play in the church. Peter became a foundational figure in the early Christian community and a leader among the apostles. The name Peter was a symbol of his strength, steadfastness, and leadership within the church.

Saul Is Renamed Paul
In the New Testament, Saul was renamed by Jesus to Paul. The name Saul means 'asked for', while the name Paul means 'small' or 'humble'. Saul was a zealous persecutor of the early Christian church until he had a dramatic conversion experience on the road to Damascus, where he encountered the risen Jesus. After his conversion, Saul began to preach the gospel and became a prominent leader in the early Christian church. The name change occurred in Acts 13:9, where Saul is called Paul for the first time. It is not explicitly stated why the

name was changed, but it is thought that Paul began to use his Roman name as he began to preach to Gentiles. The name change from Saul to Paul was significant because it marked a turning point in his ministry. It symbolized his humility and his willingness to embrace a new identity in Christ. As Paul, he went on to become one of the most influential figures in the early Christian church, writing many letters that became part of the New Testament and spreading the gospel throughout the Roman Empire.

Over the last couple of years, I have been given several names from people listening to God on my behalf. Not only do each of these names resonate deeply inside my spirit, but I have been ENORMOUSLY encouraged through hearing how God sees me, and in one case I was released!

Footnote: in Daniel 1:7 Daniel, Hananiah, Mishael and Azariah were renamed by a Babylonian official in attempt to assimilate them into the local culture and society. They became Shadrach, Meshach and Abednego. However, their given names held great meaning: Hananiah means 'Yahweh is gracious', Mishael means 'Who is like God?' and Azariah means 'Yahweh has helped'. In Daniel 3 we read the story where these brave young men refused to bow to a golden image that King Nebuchadnezzar made. They were cast into a raging furnace as a result, but miraculously survived. Their names prophetically announced the incomparable God who would graciously help them!

Now Search Out the Matter

1. Look up your names and consider their meaning.

2. Have you experienced a fresh encounter with God?

3. Take some time to ask God what name He calls you by – how has he renamed you?

4. Ask 2-3 friends to pray and ask God what name He has chosen for you. You may discover that you have several names!

5. Reflect on these additional names and what they teach you about yourself and your destiny.

6. Now pray for a friend - asking God for His name for them and then go and bless them with what you learned! It's such an exciting way to encourage others and you'll get an extra blessing in the process!

STRENGTH AND POWER

Your mind cannot fully comprehend my greatness,
or the unlimited power in my hands,
nor the thoughts that I have toward you
and have had for an eternity -
these are mysteries beyond you.
You were chosen before you were born!

However, I am your strength and power in everything.
Look to me for help in every situation.
I want you to come to know me in this way,
so that you'll always be able to face what is in front of you,
and to break through those things,
which, on the face of them, seem impossible.

I am your possible.
I am your strength.
I am your power.

It is possible for you to take hold of this truth,
to encourage you,
to build your faith,
to enable you to reach out to the vastness
of what I have made available to you
and to every child of mine.

Access my power through faith,
for the benefit of others
and you will truly enjoy all that I have for you -
amazing grace,
power beyond measure,
mercy untold
and more.

THE GLORY OF KINGS

I am an awesome God,
so do not live in fear or in captivity.
Partner with me
and see my wonders at work in your life
and in those whom you encounter.

It is all under control -
I see your struggles.
You cannot solve them all.
Don't attempt to explain everything that you encounter,
it will not help!
My timing is perfect.
Things may look hard -
sometimes impossible,
but I am here,
I have a plan,
I have a way,
I have the power,
I am the love.

With me nothing is impossible.
Declare this.
Stand on this promise.
Believe - and you will see my hands at work.
Don't carry a burden which is not yours.
If you feel a weight, it's time to pass the load to me,
I want to carry it for you,
My burden is light.
Keep your eyes fixed on me!

Now Search Out the Matter

1. When is God's strength made perfect? Find and record a verse which answers this question.

2. Who or what is said to have had power in the following verses:
   a. Deuteronomy 34:10-12
   b. Joshua 4:19-24
   c. 1 Samuel 10:5-7
   d. 1 Chronicles 29:10-13
   e. Matthew 3:11
   f. Acts 1:8
   g. Romans 1:16
   h. 1 Corinthians 4:18-20
   i. 2 Corinthians 10:3-4
   j. Ephesians 1:19-20

3. Meditate on 2 Corinthians 4:7-10. What do you learn?

4. How can we see more of God's power in our lives?

WONDER

- ❖ Chosen And Unique
- ❖ It's Ridiculous
- ❖ Tapestry
- ❖ Numbers
- ❖ Time
- ❖ Logos
- ❖ Rhema

'Finish then, Thy new creation;
Pure and spotless let us be;
Let us see Thy great salvation
Perfectly restored in Thee;
Changed from glory into glory
Till with Thee we take our place,
Till we cast our crowns before Thee,
Lost in wonder love and praise.'

Charles Wesley

CHOSEN AND UNIQUE

You are not just anybody.
You have been hand-picked.
I chose you – yes you!
You are my special possession.
You are unique.
No-one has ever lived, or will live, who is the same as you.
No-one else can make the contribution planted in you.
You are a one-off design,
with a unique purpose.
You are the missing jigsaw piece.

Everyone that I've chosen is a part of my body.
My body is my bride.
Grow into your full identity, and you will lack nothing.

I have made you a minister.
I have made you a partner.
I've made you a messenger of reconciliation.
You are a royal priest.
You are my child.
I have adopted you.

I have carefully considered those whom I have chosen.
I did not make a mistake.
I have given you everything that pertains to life and godliness.
I have shared my eternal riches with you – every blessing in the heavenly places!
I have poured out my mercy and grace on you.
I have created you in my image.
I have longed and yearned for you.
I take delight in every moment with you.
I long for your complete transformation to be like my Son.
I rejoice at your surrender.
I delight in you as you die to self.
I lift you up when you have fallen.

THE GLORY OF KINGS

I hold you when you need love.
I heal you when you are wounded.
I restore you when you are broken and hurting.

When you lose sight of me, I draw you to myself.
I surround you with my love.
I stand in front of you.
I hold out my hands to you.
I draw you to myself.
I embrace you
until you are ready
to be let go,
to walk on the path again.

I go before you.
I walk beside you.
I follow behind you to protect you.
I, Almighty God, dwell within you.
I stand at a distance and draw you to myself.
I gently nudge you back onto the path.

Do you still not understand just how much I love you,
my son, my daughter?

…you have so much more to understand,
But I will lead you and show you.
You have many more riches to acquire,
that are already laid out on a table for you -
you only have to ask
and I will give them to you.
Do not doubt my words.
Just come in simple faith.
Delight my heart.
Live in me.
Rest in my presence.
Stay a while.
Live in the fear of the Lord…

...And you will be rich beyond all measure...

In grace,
In mercy,
In hope,
In love,
In joy,
In peace.

My Son died to make all this possible.
You are blessed to be chosen.
You are blessed to be my child.

Now Search Out the Matter

1. Ask three close friends to describe ways in which you are unique.

2. What responsibility does our uniqueness place on us?

3. What might this imply about our destiny?

IT'S RIDICULOUS

I thought about you from the beginning of time.
I created you for my glory.
You are fearfully and wonderfully made.
I know every cell in your body.
I perceive every thought that you have.
I see every movement that you make.
You are beautiful in my sight.

It's ridiculous!

I think about you all the time.
My gaze rests upon you each day.
I wait in excitement for you.
I long to be with you.
I have readied a new gift for our next encounter.
It's been uniquely designed for your needs.
It's designed to be used for my glory.

It's ridiculous!

I knew our relationship would be broken.
I wept at the thought of separation from you.
My heart was broken.
I determined to win you back,
whatever the cost.
I laid out the greatest plan in history
and prepared the ultimate sacrifice.

It's ridiculous!

THE GLORY OF KINGS

I loved you from the outset.
I couldn't help it –
it's who I am.
Nothing persuaded me to change my divine plan -
nor did your failures that I foresaw,
nor did the pain that I knew you would cause me.
I was overwhelmed by inextinguishable love for you.

It's ridiculous!

I yearned for your love.
I gave everything to draw you back.
I waited patiently until you were ready.
I revealed the truth to your heart.
I convicted you of folly.
I rejoiced at your response
and embraced you with all that I am.

It's ridiculous!

I made you completely new.
I washed away your past, present and future failure.
I chose to dwell in you.
I shared my eternal riches with you.
I gave you everything you needed.
I changed you from one degree of glory to another -
and I'm still reshaping and transforming you!

It's ridiculous!

That same love surrounds you today.
That same love fills you today.
That same love restores you today.
That same love provides for you today.
That same love beckons you today.
That same love welcomes you into my presence today.
That same love makes you more beautiful today.

It's ridiculous!

This is all just too wonderful, deep, and incomprehensible!

How can this be both divine and ridiculous at the same time?

Well, it only makes sense when you consider....

The unthinkable excess,
the unimaginable vastness,
the expansive extravagance,
the boundless enormity,
the infinite generosity and
the overwhelming abundance,
of my love for you.

And yet - even now - you *still* do not understand just how much I love you!!!

Now Search Out the Matter

1. What other words would you use instead of 'ridiculous' to describe God's love for you?

2. Make a list of all the ways God has shown you His love in the last month, then give thanks for each moment.

3. Write a list of the ways you can demonstrate your love for God. What actions will you take now?

TAPESTRY

My child,

You see my hand?
It's always been on you.
I've heard you discussing the wonderful tapestry which I've
created throughout your life -
how I have woven together the path that you've taken
with the path of many others.
How I have brought the right people to you –
just at the right time - and you see correctly!

Now you understand the truth of my words to you:
that I will never fail you nor forsake you,
that I do have plans for your good,
that your destiny is clear.

You are beginning to see the path that I've laid before you
and how that path is woven into my universal plan,
into my Kingdom.
I will not leave you directionless.
I will not step away.
I will not abandon you.

I've been keeping you protected.
As you walk in the centre of my will -
my wings wrap around you and protect you.
My words guide you.
The light of my glory reveals your path!

You will not come to harm.
You need never live in fear.
Even though I call you to be transformed
and to keep stepping out of the safety of the boat,
always remember to keep your eyes on me –
not on the storm.

THE GLORY OF KINGS

If you will listen to me, trust me, and obey me immediately,
you will never wander like the children of Israel,
lost in the desert.
If you always keep your eyes fixed on me
and trust my words,
and look to me for what you need,
you will discover over and over,
that I AM Jehovah Jireh, God your provider!

If you spend time with me, and listen
and take care with what I give you,
then you will be truly blessed.
You will experience the abundance of my goodness.
You will perceive my continued faithfulness in your life.
You will be moved to thanksgiving and praise!

I have set an open door before you.
Do not hesitate.
Go straight on through.
The vista may seem strange at first
and the perspective will assuredly be new!

The path may look different -
but know this, my child,
I have already walked it!
I have already purposed it!
I have already seen you moving along it!
I know where it leads.
I designed you for this specific route.
There is no need to fear.
I will not fail you.
I will not let you down – ever!
You have no cause for worry or anxiety.
All I ask is that you take the next step
and the next step
and the next step
and keep moving with me.

THE GLORY OF KINGS

At times, I will be right beside you.
At times, you will see me up ahead -
keep walking in that direction.
On other occasions,
you will just sense that I am behind you.
You will always know me within you.
Listen only to my voice.

And whilst you may enjoy what you see as you travel,
or at times be intimidated by what surrounds you,
know this for sure -
that you are my beloved child
and I will NOT let you come to harm.

My continual delight is to see you trust in me.
My continual wish for you,
is that you surrender to my will…
Everything.
Every day.
Every hour.
Every moment.

I have things I would like to say to you.
Are you prepared to turn yourself to me?
Can you hear what I'm saying? Are you listening?
Have you stilled your mind long enough?
Have you cast all your cares on me?
Have you remembered all that I have spoken to you?
These thoughts will lead you in a way of peace
and keep you in the place of peace,
When you are fully at rest, you will hear me speak clearly.

I will reveal myself to you.
I will give you knowledge.
I will explain mysteries to you.
I will unveil new things about my character:
things you have never thought about,

things that you cannot imagine today.

You are part of my beautiful bride.
Take every step that you can,
to be ready for when I come to fetch you –
to bring you home!

In the meantime,
some of the backcloth is still bare,
more of my beautiful tapestry will be woven into your life,
into the glorious picture that I am creating in you.
Keep your eyes open, so you don't miss it!

Now Search Out the Matter

1. Having read the above, are there any statements that significant for you, or what you need to hear right now? Reflect on these.

2. Reflect on your life to date and write down the special things that God has done for you, in you, and through you. The more time you spend doing this the more you will see!

3. Now ask Holy Spirit to show you what you missed!

4. Read the short book of Ruth and write down how God made a way for an unmarried, foreign widow in Israel (who so being would find life very hard) to be restored to happiness. Note how and why God rewards each of the key characters. Then consider how God uses the events of this apparently insignificant story to fulfil His long-term plan for world redemption.

NUMBERS

How big is your God?

John 1:3 *'Through Him all things were made; without Him nothing was made that has been made'*

100,000,000,000 stars in our galaxy
10,000,000,000,000 galaxies, thus…
1,000,000,000,000,000,000,000,000 stars in the universe

Psalm 147:4 *'He determines the number of the stars and calls them* **each by name**'

In comparison to the number of stars (one septillion, per the above) that He can name, only 117,000,000,000 people have **ever** lived - therefore He has no problem in remembering your name, and every detail of your life!

Psalm 139:14 *'I praise you because I am fearfully and wonderfully made; your works are wonderful - I know that full well'*

100,000,000,000,000 atoms per cell
100,000,000,000,000 cells in the body
10,000,000,000,000,000,000,000,000,000 atoms in the body
1,500,000,000,000,000,000,000 molecules in a drop of water
20,000,000,000,000,000,000,000,000 molecules in the human body (>99% of which are water)
Over 200 bones and 600 muscles in your body,
100's of nerves and billions of neurons.
100 billion neurons in your brain alone!

Matthew 10:30 *'And even the very hairs of your head are all numbered'*

100,000 hairs on your head
8,000,000,000 people on earth
800,000,000,000,000 hairs numbered by Him today!

Psalm 139 17-18 *'How precious to me are your thoughts, God! How vast is the sum of them! Were I to count them, they would outnumber the grains of sand'*

His thoughts about you exceed the…
7,500,000,000,000,000,000 grains of sand on earth

You have 6,000 thoughts per day, and thus circa 175,000,000 in your lifetime,

And thus,
He has over 40 billion times as many thoughts about you than the total that you think in a lifetime…

…are all your thoughts about Him?

Note to the reader: all the above numbers, obtained from the internet are by nature estimates at best. Most, even if incorrect by a significant factor, should still evoke a huge sense of amazement and awe in you!! Don't get bogged down in the numbers and miss the point!

Now Search Out the Matter

Now it's your turn to explore some numbers and use the journey to expand your view of the **infinite** character of God! Use the internet (or your local library) as an exploration tool. In each case consider what you learn about the Creator? Find Biblical text(s) to link your thoughts to.

1. How many fish are in our oceans? How many species have been identified? Make a comparison with the number of birds. Why such a difference?

2. How many times does a human heart beat in an average lifespan? How does that compare to the robustness and longevity of things man has created?

3. Explore the complexity of the human hand. How many of each element are there in the hand (e.g. bones, muscles, nerves, arteries, veins). What does this imply about the Creator's intention for our hands?

4. How many nerves connect to the human eye? How many nerve fibres is the optic nerve comprised of? What percentage of the brain's cortex is devoted to visual processing?

5. Take some time to worship our amazing Creator!

TIME

Is time kept in heaven? Is it a dimension in heaven? Genesis 1:1-3 indicates earthly time began with creation.

What existed or happened before or at the beginning of time? Read the following verses and note what you discover:

    Titus 1:2..

    John 1:1..

    1 Peter 1:18-20......................................

    Ephesians 1:4...

    Proverbs 8:22...

    2 Timothy 1:9..

    John 17:5...

What is God's perspective on time when compared with our own? In 2 Peter 3:8 we read:

'But do not forget this one thing, dear friends: with the Lord a day is like a thousand years, and a thousand years are like a day'

The former expression of time would mean that a day for God encompasses 40 generations on earth! The latter expression of time would mean that a year for God passes in 1 minute 26.4 seconds!!

I think it's safe to assume God is outside of time. Revelation 1:8 and Revelation 21:6 teach us that Jesus is both the first and the last – 'Alpha and Omega', the beginning and end of all things, from eternity past to eternity future. This theme appears in Colossians 1:18 too.

There are two Greek words in the New Testament for time: Chronos (χρόνος) and Kairos (καιρός).

Chronos refers to chronological or sequential time. It is quantitative and is measured in seconds, minutes, hours, days and years using clocks and calendars. It expresses the relative position of events in our lives, in our time.

Kairos, on the other hand, is qualitative. It indicates the right or critical moment, the opportune time for action, the fitting season, the suitable time. Kairos can be considered as referring to God's timing within His plan. For us it is about making the most of the moment, seizing the day appointed by God.

By way of illustration, here are some verses where Kairos is used:

'The time has come,' he said. 'The kingdom of God has come near. Repent and believe the good news!'
Mark 1:15

'He made known to us the mystery of his will according to his good pleasure, which he purposed in Christ, to be put into effect when the times reach their fulfilment – to bring unity to all things in heaven and on earth under Christ.'
Ephesians 1:9-10

'Therefore, as we have opportunity, let us do good to all people, especially to those who belong to the family of believers.'
Galatians 6:10

'Be very careful, then, how you live – not as unwise but as wise, making the most of every opportunity, because the days are evil.'

Ephesians 5:15-16

Time is an irretrievable resource – once elapsed it cannot be regained. It is thus of immense value and we should regard it with due respect and diligence. Our concept of time differs from that from God's perspective and we need to keep His eternal viewpoint in mind at all times!

Now Search Out the Matter

1. Write a sentence embracing all the things that occurred before or at the beginning of time. What is the eternal impact of these things?

2. Looking at 2 Peter 3:8, can you now see God's perspective at a time when God's answer to your prayer seemed to take forever? Was the moment it came about a Chronos or Kairos event?

3. Should we concern ourselves, or debate with one another, to pin down unrevealed times? Read Matthew 24. Are you watching? Are you ready? Are you making the most of every opportunity?

4. There are two words about time found in Ecclesiastes 3: one appears once, the other on 28 occasions. Are these Hebrew equivalents to Kairos and Chronos?

5. Read Esther 4:14. Are you in a position 'for a time such as this?'

LOGOS

The living, *written*, entire, eternal, immutable word of God.

The table below lists verses in which the Greek word Logos (λόγος) is used.

Logos Characteristic	Reference
Of the Kingdom	Matthew 13:19
Eternal	Matthew 24:35
Gracious	Luke 4:22
Authoritative	Luke 4:32
Powerful	Luke 4:36
From the beginning	John 1:1
God	John 1:1
With God	John 1:1
Became flesh	John 1:14
The Father's	John 14:24
Truth	John 17:17
Sent by God	Acts 10:36
Spreading and flourishing	Acts 12:24
Of salvation	Acts 13:26
Spoken by the prophets	Acts 15:15
Wisdom and knowledge	1 Corinthians 12:8
Dwelling in us	Colossians 3:16
Nourishing	1 Timothy 4:6
Alive, active, and sharp	Hebrews 4:12
Penetrating, judging	Hebrews 4:12
Our accountability	Hebrews 4:13
Planted in us	James 1:21
Living in us	1 John 2:14
Jesus' name	Revelation 19:13

Now Search Out the Matter

1. In John 1:1-5 do you find any separation or difference between the 'Word' and 'Jesus'? Read these verses again out loud, but this time replace 'Word' with 'Jesus' as you read.

2. Read Genesis 1 and note down how many times the words 'God said' appear. What is the link between what God said and creation? How powerful is what He says? What is the connection found in John 1:3 between the spoken word of God, Jesus and creation?

3. How much power is implied when God speaks?

4. Now read Proverbs 18:20-21. What is the power of our spoken words? Is the power of our words related in any way to being made in the image of God?

5. Read Hebrews 4:12-13 in several different versions. Is it your testimony that the Word of God is alive, active and sharp in your life?

RHEMA

The freshly *spoken* word of God with power to fulfil itself.

The table below lists verses in which the Greek word Rhema (ῥῆμα) is used.

Rhema Characteristic	Reference
Spoken by God	Matthew 4:4
Prophetic	Matthew 26:75
Unfailing	Luke 1:37
To an individual	Luke 3:2
Jesus' words	Luke 24:8
Full of the Spirit	John 6:63
Full of life	John 6:63
Of eternal life	John 6:68
Those who belong to God	John 8:47
From the Father	John 14:10
To remain in us	John 15:7
Given to Jesus by the Father	John 17:8
Preaching	Acts 10:37
Holy Spirit moves when spoken	Acts 10:44
Nearby	Romans 10:8
In your mouth and heart	Romans 10:8
Faith comes by hearing it	Romans 10:17
Cleansing	Ephesians 5:26
The sword of the Spirit	Ephesians 6:17
Powerful	Hebrews 1:3
Good	Hebrews 6:5
Creative	Hebrews 11:3
Eternal	1 Peter 1:25

Now Search Out the Matter

1. Review the two preceding tables (Logos and Rhema). Note down the similarities. Then note down the differences.

2. Are there any characteristics in the Logos table which are not immediately identifiable as - or synonymous with - Jesus?

3. Which members of the Godhead are identifiable within the Rhema table?

4. When God speaks to you in your quiet place, is this Logos or Rhema or both?

5. For decades I assumed (was even taught by implication) that 'the sword of the Spirit, which is the word of God' (Ephesians 6:17) was the Bible (Logos). I now know the Greek word here is Rhema. What then is the 'sword of the Spirit'?

6. Write down three Rhema that you have received and check if you have seen them fulfilled in your life. If you don't think you have received a Rhema word, then ask Holy Spirit to bring you one.

THE CROSS

- ❖ Freedom
- ❖ The Staging Of Salvation
- ❖ Fragrance
- ❖ 39 Lashes Of Love
- ❖ What Am I?
- ❖ In Remembrance
- ❖ Inheritance

*'When Jesus hung on the Cross,
a great unseen cosmic battle raged in the
heavens – and in the end,
Christ triumphed over all the forces of evil
and death and hell.'*

Billy Graham

FREEDOM

You need to know that there's a place
where you can find complete freedom -
It's at the foot of the Cross.
The Cross marks the place where freedom was secured -
for everyone!

It is here that the journey begins.
Nothing can hinder the power of the Cross.
It brings lasting salvation and freedom.
It reveals the extent of my love -
the lengths that I went to,
in order that I could purchase what was necessary
to liberate all those enslaved by sin, guilt, and shame -
everyone!

The price is paid -
there is no outstanding debt.
No burden of the past to carry.
A gift freely given.
To everyone!

Now you must accept the gift -
then allow it to permeate your mind
and transform it.
There is healing, cleansing, restoration
and freedom at the Cross
for everyone!

Many need to come
and many need to return,
to the foot of the Cross,
to see, or remember, what I have done for them -
what I want to do for them.
My blood was poured out to bring freedom from death -
the place where I am not.

The Cross is a fountain of grace and mercy,
where all can come and be cleansed -
where all can come to drink and be refreshed.
No-one is excluded.
I will draw my chosen to me.
Stand in peace at the foot of the Cross
and consider all that I have done for you.
The truth will set you free!

The place of the Cross is very special in the Kingdom.
It is at the core of your redemption.
My Son's blood given as a sacrifice for you.
His body broken for you.
Death conquered.
Grace released.
Mercy overflowing.
The curtain torn in two.
Peace flowing freely from heaven to earth.

Never lose sight of this wonderful gift.
Abundant life, freedom, peace, and joy.
All earned through Jesus' death,
none of it secured by you.
The highest price has been paid.
Now truly live in this freedom.
Sin no more.
Live worthy of the death that brought you eternal life.

Now Search Out the Matter

Answer the following by searching out a relevant verse or passage of scripture:

1. What is the purpose of freedom?

2. What sets us free?

3. Who sets us free?

4. What have you been freed from?

5. What have you been freed to do?

6. How certain is your freedom?

7. Ask Holy Spirit if there is any area you need freeing from.

THE STAGING OF SALVATION

Props	Cast	Lead Actor
Swords *Clubs* False evidence *Spit* Fists *Hands* A flesh-ripping scourge *A prison* A crown of thorns *A purple robe* A tree *Cruel nails* A hammer *A notice* The place of a skull *A spear* A tomb *A large stone* 30 pieces of silver *The temple curtain*	*Sleepy friends* A traitor *Soldiers* Officials *High Priest's servant* Chief priests and elders *False witnesses* A fisherman in denial *The High Priest* Jewish leaders *A weak Roman Governor* A company of Roman soldiers *The Jews* An insurrectionist and murderer *Teachers of the law* A foreigner from Cyrene *Soldiers* An insulting mob	Jesus *Son to Mary and Joseph* A 33 year-old *Carpenter* Son of Man *Son of God* King of the Jews *Beloved Son* Lamb of God *Saviour* Redeemer *Bread of life* Lord *Creator* Holy One of Israel *King of Kings* Head of the church *The Almighty* Alpha and Omega *Master* High Priest *Prophet* Teacher *Immanuel*

Props	Cast	Lead Actor
	A grieving mother An aunt *Women* A best friend *Frightened followers* Two condemned rebels *A wise centurion* A rich man	Advocate *Mediator* Judge *Cornerstone* Good Shepherd *The Word* Fountain of living waters *Rock* True vine *Righteousness* Branch *Bridegroom* Lion of Judah *Bright Morning Star* The Way *The Truth* The Life *Christ* **Your Messiah**

Now Search Out the Matter

Select a **'prop'**.
- What part does it play in the story?
   - Consider the impact it had on Jesus.
   - Think how it would have affected you
   - What does it teach you about Jesus and how He suffered?

1. Choose a **'cast member'**.
   - What part did they play?
   - What was their angle on the events that took place?
   - What was their error?
   - How did Jesus respond to them?
   - Might you have been like them in the same situation? - Is there any similarity to the way that you have sometimes been treated?
   -What was your reaction?

2. Pick a title of the **'lead actor'**.
   - Write a full description of that title
   - Now consider how that characteristic of Jesus impacts you today
   - Finish by offering up thanks and praise for who He is to you!

FRAGRANCE

I'm called Nardostachys Jatamansi, a flowering plant, part of the valerian family, growing in the Himalayas of India and Nepal at an altitude of between 3000 and 5000 metres. I am pink in colour, bell-shaped, aromatic and I'm sometimes known as muskroot.

My underground stems and leaves can be crushed and distilled into an intensely aromatic amber coloured oil which contains the full essence of my fragrance.

I was traded across the ancient world and imported by the Romans and Jews, at great expense, to be used as a perfumed ointment. I had been placed in an alabaster jar and loaded on the back of a donkey along with other goods. A caravan of traders then embarked on the long, slow and arduous journey across the rugged terrain of Central Asia and the Middle East until we eventually arrived in Jerusalem.

In my case I was sold by my trader to a shop close to the marketplace in Jerusalem, which specialised in perfumes and a wide range of scented oils and other aromatic products.

A young woman travelled the two miles to Jerusalem from Bethany specifically to purchase perfume. She invested almost a year's wages to acquire me before carrying her purchase home. I expected to be on the shelf of that shop much longer given that very few could afford me.

But then the strangest things happened – I was poured over someone's feet rather than adorning the young woman's neck and cheeks – and stranger still, it was she that indulged in this peculiar act – made yet more incredulous when she wiped his feet with her beautiful long flowing hair.

As my fragrance filled the entire house an argument broke out. 'Why had I been wasted?', after all, I was worth a fortune! Still, everyone knew about my presence then as my scent filled the home…

…and I too identified an incredible fragrance unlike any that I had ever sensed in the place where I was prepared, or in the shop where I was sold. It was a divine fragrance arising from the person on whom I had been poured, a beautiful presence in the room like none other I had ever experienced.

And then, adding to the mystery of the moment, the man, on whose feet I had been poured, announced that this act had been an embalming in preparation for his burial, even though he was alive and well?

From India,
   to Jerusalem,
      to Bethany,
         to a family home,
           to a cross,
              to a grave,
                 for a death infinitely more valuable than I

The oil from crushed stems and leaves was poured out on the very one who was crushed and who poured Himself out for all.

Now, as a result….

'…we are to God the pleasing aroma of Christ among those who are being saved and those who are perishing. To the one we are an aroma that brings death; to the other, an aroma that brings life'

2 Corinthians 2:15-16

Now Search Out the Matter

1. Imagine you were either the woman or an onlooker:
   - See yourself in the scene
   - What were your reactions?
   - What emotions did you feel?

2. In Exodus 30:22-29, God gives Moses instructions on how to make a special anointing oil. What ingredients were used? What is the Biblical symbolism for each one?

3. Investigate what perfumes are likened to in Song of Songs 1:3.

4. In Psalm 45 who is being described? What do the anointing oils signify here (v8)?

39 LASHES OF LOVE

I always want to repress the images in my head of Jesus being scourged – a Roman punishment that took a man within inches of death. But for a moment, allow the physical pain, and the injustice of that torture to touch you, and then ask Holy Spirit to invade your spirit with a true understanding of the love, cost and purpose for which Christ endured this for you as prophesied in Isaiah 53:5.

#1 Healed
#2   through love revealed
#3 Renewed
#4   in love pursued
#5 Made whole
#6   by a spotless soul
#7 Mended
#8   by grace resplendent
#9 Revived
#10   so we survived
#11 Repaired
#12   because He cared
#13 Strengthened
#14   by His intention
#15 Soothed
#16   with pain removed
#17 Cleansed
#18   via agony intense
#19 Restored
#20   as blood was poured
#21 Redeemed
#22   as bloody sweat streamed
#23 Forgiven
#24   and bound for heaven
#25 Made heirs
#26   through flesh-ripped tears

#27 Filled
#28   because blood spilled
#29 Released
#30   bringing peace
#31 Freed
#32   though a broken reed
#33 Delivered
#34   as His body withered
#35 Resurrected
#36   and forever protected
#37 Gifted eternity
#38   through His humility
#39 By His stripes we are healed

Imagine the pain.
Consider the cost.
Fathom the love.
A gift at the highest price.
Give thanks again and again.
Cast out demons,
Heal the sick,
Raise the dead,
Cleanse the lepers.

Now Search Out the Matter

1. Ask Holy Spirit to show you the unopened gifts made available to you through Jesus' obedience and agony, then hold out your hands to receive them.

2. List 39 blessings that you have received, for which He paid the ultimate price out of love for you. Use the table below to do this. I have started you off…

	He Was…	So That I Could Be…
1	Despised	Loved
2	Rejected	Accepted
3	Familiar with pain	
4		
5		
6		
7		
8		
9		
10		
11		
12		
13		
14		
15		
16		
17		
18		
19		
20		
21		

THE GLORY OF KINGS

22		
23		
24		
25		
26		
27		
28		
29		
30		
31		
32		
33		
34		
35		
36		
37		
38		
39	Lashed	Lavished with love

WHAT AM I?

In ancient Rome I was typically made by hand using iron or bronze. The process of making me was quite laborious and involved several steps.

First the metal I was to be made from was heated until it was red hot. Then the blacksmith used tongs to hold the metal and a hammer to shape me into the desired form. This involved flattening one end and then forming a point at the other end. Once I had been shaped, I was cooled and hardened by being plunged into water. After I had cooled, any rough edges or burrs were filed down to make me smooth and easier to use for the purpose I was made.

This process of making me was time-consuming and required a great deal of skill, so I was relatively expensive and typically used sparingly. In fact, it was very common for me to be reused as a result. In my case I was taken in hand for a brutal execution in a method intended to be slow, tortuous, inhumane and humiliating. I would pin a hand or a foot to wood, preventing the victim from escape whilst inflicting agonizing pain.

Once the cruel objective had been achieved, I'd be removed and stored in readiness for re-use with the next criminal or traitor, since I was a valuable resource to my owner.

I did not choose my purpose or design, but I'll never forget being driven through the right hand of the Son of God.

Was it your hand on the hammer?

Now Search Out the Matter

1. Now try this approach yourself. You can choose any Bible story or object, then use your imagination and the passage, or commentaries, to write about it from a new perspective. If you are stuck for ideas, here are a few:

   - Towel (John 13)
   - Myrrh (Matthew 2)
   - Mat (Mark 2)

2. Try seeing a Biblical situation through the eyes of one of the characters involved. Write about what they might have been thinking. If you are stuck for ideas, here are a few characters whose heads you could 'get inside of':

   - Nicodemus (John 3)
   - Naaman (2 Kings 5)
   - Centurion (Luke 7)
   - Judas (Matthew 27)

IN REMEMBRANCE

"And he took bread, gave thanks and broke it, and gave it to them, saying, 'This is my body given for you; do this in remembrance of me.' In the same way, after the supper he took the cup, saying, 'This cup is the new covenant in my blood, which is poured out for you.'" (Luke 22:19-20).

What follows is a meditation based on Matthew 26 and 27.

Betrayed by one so close.
Denied by a best friend and
accused without cause.
Spat on.
Struck with fists.
Slapped by hands, then
charged with blasphemy.

Quizzed by the governor.
Accused by the priests, yet
silent in defence.
Denied release by a mob.
Taken captive whilst a criminal walked free.
Disowned by an ineffectual judge then
flogged close to death.

Stripped and dressed in scarlet.
Crowned with a twist of thorns.
Handed a staff as a sceptre and
mocked as a king.
Spat on in disdain.
Beaten with a stick then
crucified on a cross.

THE GLORY OF KINGS

>Lots cast for his clothes.
>Watched over in contempt.
>Charged as an earthly king and
>insulted by rebels.
>Scorned by the religious.
>Decried as the Son of God and then
>forsaken by his father.

In 1910 John Wilbur Chapman wrote a beautiful hymn, the chorus of which I sang many times as a child. He used so few words so beautifully and so succinctly to embrace the entire Gospel:

>'Living he loved you,
>Dying He saved you,
>Buried He carried,
>Your sins far away.
>Rising He justified,
>Freely forever,
>Some day He's coming,
>Oh Glorious day!'

Now Search Out the Matter

Read Matthew 26 and 27, on which the meditation 'In Remembrance' is based.

- Is there anything that has taken place in your life that Jesus also faced in the last days before He died?

- How did He respond?

- How should you respond?

- Do you need healing in this matter?

- Do you believe Jesus both understands what you have been through and can heal or restore you?

INHERITANCE

Child of God, *Prophet & Loss Solicitors*
Earth, *Heaven,*
2 DAY *AD 33*
  Date: Kairos Moment

Dear Child of God,

Re: Last Will & (New) Testament of Jesus of Nazareth

It is with mixed feelings that I am bound to write to you at this time. I write, given you were not present at His passing, and in the knowledge that you have read, but not yet fully understood His Will.

I am pleased to write to advise you that I have now completed the administration of the above estate. Please find enclosed:

- A cheque for the sum of £ Eternal:Life
- A copy of the original and the upgraded will
- A copy of the final estate accounts
- A form of receipt

Please sign and return the enclosed receipt to me as soon as possible.

Yours sincerely,

Archangel Trust Worthy
(διαχείριση)

Encl. Original and Upgraded Wills
(Old and New Testaments)

Final Estate Accounts

Income
(*Acquired By You*)

Glory
Divine Adoption
Infinite Riches
Eternal Life
His Presence
His Power
Trinity Fellowship
Righteousness
Healing & Restoration
A Part In His Plan
Freedom From Sin

Expenditure
(*Relinquished by Him*)

Heavenly Glory
His Divinity
Infinite Riches
Immortality
Omnipresence
Omnipotence
Father's Fellowship
His Reputation
A Painless Existence
His Will
His Life

Notes:
a. In the above, all expenditure and costs in coming to earth have been paid by the deceased. There is nothing outstanding. An immeasurable income has been left to you as indicated.
b. Considerable detail of your new benefits can be found in His will.
c. The above is conditional on your acceptance of His sacrifice and lordship.

Contact: angelmail@heaven.come

Now Search Out the Matter

1. Write a reply to the above letter expressing your joy at receiving such an inheritance!

2. Make a list of as many further benefits as you can - see Note (b) above.

3. Is there anyone that you need to share your inheritance with? Plan to do this!

THE GLORY OF KINGS

WORSHIP

- Worship And Surrender
- Worship
- Remember
- Idols
- Majesty
- A Crescendo Of Worship
- Victory Amplified

*'True worship is not a performance,
but a lifestyle.
The closer we get to God,
the more we will hate sin.
If there is no wind of the Spirit,
the church is just a pile of dry bones.'*

A.W. Tozer

WORSHIP AND SURRENDER

I have a question - for which I have no definitive answer - if indeed there is one!

> Is worship a form of surrender,
> or is surrender a form of worship?

I've thought about this a lot, not because I must know the answer, but rather because I wanted to understand more about each. Some readers may see little value in resolving this question – that's ok - I simply want to provoke you to think over and develop your own viewpoint on this. It's often the process of 'seeking out a matter' that yields the value, rather than just the discovery of a 'right answer'. So here are some thoughts to chew on!

Surrender – a form of Worship?

In essence, worship is about the act of subscribing honour, reverence and adoration to God. It involves acknowledging His worthiness, falling prostrate before Him, recognising His love for us and thanking Him for everything He has done for us and given to us. We are to glorify God, no-one else, and especially not ourselves. As we worship, we acknowledge our absolute dependency on Him, our smallness, our weakness, our absolute need for Him – and by contrast His greatness, His mercy, His strength and His love. In John 15:5 Jesus reminds that 'apart from me you can do nothing.'

Worship involves an intimate connection with God – the bliss of communion with Him. Jeremiah 29:13 tells us that 'You will seek me and find me when you seek me with all your heart.' Ephesians 2:6 reminds us of the incredible privilege that we have 'God raised us up with Christ and seated us with him in the heavenly realms in Christ Jesus.' And then there is the beautiful invitation in Revelation 3:20, 'Here I am! I stand at the door and knock. If anyone hears my voice and opens the door, I will come in and eat with that person, and they with me.'

Worship has the power to transform and renew us as we worship. As we focus on God's majesty and holiness, our hearts and minds are reshaped, aligning us more closely with His will. Romans 12:1 emphasizes this transformative aspect of worship: 'Therefore, I urge you, brothers and sisters, in view of God's mercy, to offer your bodies as a living sacrifice, holy and pleasing to God—this is your true and proper worship.'

Worship may take different forms. Our minds tend to go straight to praise and thanksgiving. However, prayer and intercession form another aspect of worship. Likewise, reflection on and obedience to what He has revealed through His Word constitute worship. Participating in sacraments such as baptism and communion also serve as tangible expressions of worship, reminding us of Christ's sacrifice and our salvation.

Thus, we see that worship encompasses reverence and awe, gratitude and thankfulness, praise, authenticity and sincerity, unity and fellowship, surrender and obedience.

All this might suggest that surrender is a form of worship.

Worship – a form of Surrender?

Surrender requires us to yield control of our lives, relinquish our plans, hand over our desires and let go of our will. John 3:30 indicates a change of perspective is required 'He must become greater; I must become less'. Recognising He is greater is to recognise His sovereignty, His worthiness, His Lordship, His wisdom, His power, His purpose and His plan. Surrender requires us to come into alignment with God, not the reverse! Failure to surrender reflects either rebellion or a misunderstanding of His character and trustworthiness.

Surrendering to God paves the way for a closer relationship with Him. In surrendering we accept His plan is best for us. Our surrender demonstrates that we acknowledge that we were created to worship Him. Worship entails the complete surrender of our bodies as 'a living sacrifice, holy and pleasing to God – this is your true and proper worship' (Romans 12:1).

Surrender requires faith – as we let go of what we are holding onto, He always catches us. As we let go, our self-dependency decreases and simultaneously our security increases as He holds us safe. When we let go, we meet the God who 'never fails us or forsakes us.'

I have often carried a burden that I didn't need to. At times I have released a load to Him, and subsequently taken it back on my shoulders. Surrender is never a one-off action. It should, however, be a lifestyle. Jesus invites us: 'Come to me, all you who are weary and burdened, and I will give you rest' (Matthew 11:28). Passing Him our burdens and taking on his yoke (Matthew 11:29) is an act of regular surrender and brings relief.

I learned recently that when Jesus quotes Isaiah 61:1 (in Luke 4:18 'The Spirit of the Lord is on me') that the word 'on' or 'upon' when used can mean 'yoke'. Paraphrasing using this idea we have 'The Spirit of the Lord is yoked to me'!!! Thus, when Jesus says, 'Take my yoke upon you' in Matthew 11:29, we could write 'Live yoked to my Spirit'!

So if we want to truly worship in 'Spirit and in Truth', the key is surrendering to, and being yoked to the Spirit.

Now Search Out the Matter

---

1. What did you conclude? Worship is part of surrender or vice versa?

2. Is 'a great time of worship' about how well the band played, or the melodies, or the lyrics, or how you felt? If not, what is it about? Write a short paragraph using what you've learned to describe what worship and surrender look like for you?

3. Is worship a lifestyle for you? Is surrender a lifestyle for you? What needs to change?

4. What do you need to surrender?

5. What does worshipping Him in Spirit and truth look like to you? John 4:23

6. What does living 'yoked to Holy Spirit' look like to you?

WORSHIP

A few years ago, I was reading a book that encouraged me to ask God 'what does my worship look like to you? What would you like it to look like?' As I listened to Holy Spirit back then I journaled what I heard. As I re-read my journal, further thoughts came to mind:

"You are welcome here!
You stand in my presence, in my courts.
It is a place for you to re-orient your mind,
to reset and release your praise,
to rest in and receive my peace.

Worship from you is like a new morning,
with fresh dew on the forest floor,
releasing a beautiful fragrance.

It's you, lifting your heart to me,
surrendering yourself once again,
to my love and
to my Kingship.

It's the beautiful sound of your words of praise.
It's you, recalling all that I have done for you,
with thanksgiving flooding your heart.
It's you, walking by my side throughout the day,
listening and chatting and laughing together.
It's in each action of faith and obedience that you take
and every word that you speak to me.
It's all for my pleasure and glory.

The place of worship,
is where you will find fountains of living water -
to refresh you and cleanse you.
Bathe in my love.
Let it soften you.

THE GLORY OF KINGS

Let it reach your heart and reshape it.
I will make your heart tender to others.
Don't drown out my still small voice!!!
Listen, digest, and obey.
Walk with me and enjoy our time together.
Use this privilege for the benefit of others.

Take time with me.
It is the only way.
It will lead you to a new place.
There is no instant transformation…
…rather one which comes through intimacy.

Change will come, but first
you must surrender your time, your activities, your dreams,
then your heart
and all that is on your heart.
When you clear that space for me,
then you will hear me speak.
It is then that we can be together in Spirit and in truth.

Try it and you will see.
You will always find solace in me –
comfort and joy in my presence.

Be sure to come to me with everything.
Nothing is too small.
nothing is too big.
I am here for you.
I want you to hear, to understand and to act on my words,
in order that you grow in faith and wisdom.
I have so much to teach you.
Spend time with me in secret
and discover the eternal riches that I have for you.
Discover who I am,
understand my character, and my Word."

Now Search Out the Matter

1. Ask two friends what worship means to them and write their answers down.

2. Write down your definition of worship. Use a paragraph, rather than just a few words, to describe it fully.

3. Ask Holy Spirit what your worship looks like to Him. Write down the answer.

4. Now write a personal Psalm of worship. Psalms are a form of prayer and worship and cover many areas including praise, thanksgiving, lament and confession, but for this exercise concentrate on worship.

5. Now pray your Psalm each day this week.

    (If you are a musician, why not put your personal Psalm to music?)

REMEMBER

As I drove to church in the early weeks after my wife died my route took me past the hospice where she spent her final days on earth. Each time I saw the hospice sign, I would sense a heaviness and sadness descend on me. I wondered how long I could keep facing that dark reminder of her suffering. After several weeks as I drove that way again, I prayed and sensed God saying the following to me:

> *'Look up, don't look back.*
> *Keep your eyes fixed on me.*
> *Each time you pass this way,*
> *don't dwell on Katie's death,*
> *dwell on Jesus' death.'*

From that day onwards and as I approached the area where the hospice was en route to church I would pray and effectively hold a short communion service in my thoughts. Having done so, I would always arrive at church in peace rather than grief. I had stopped looking in the rear-view mirror! There's not a day that I don't miss her, but I have found peace. This episode led me to do a study investigating what the Bible taught about what we should remember.

In most cases, scripture teaches us to look up, look forward and look outwards. We are not encouraged to look backwards or to dwell on our past – however there are a few exceptions where we are called to remember. A quick analysis of the word 'remember' throughout the Bible identifies a handful of things that we are exhorted or commanded to remember: -

> The Sabbath to keep it holy
> His promises
> His commands
> That he is the Lord our God
> That he is our Creator and that there is none other like Him
> The wonders He has done
> His miracles
> His judgements
> Our leaders
> That we were once slaves and now we are free
> Jesus' sacrifice for us as we celebrate communion together

Each time we come before our Father to make requests of Him, we are to begin with a time of thanksgiving – an act of remembrance - as Philippians 4:6 reminds us:

'Do not be anxious about anything, but in every situation, by prayer and petition, with thanksgiving, present your requests to God'

Recalling His goodness and then thanking him for it builds our faith for the future and keeps our focus on the one who never fails us.

In order not to forget God's goodness and faithfulness we should also consider Jeremiah 31:21. Reading this in different versions of the Bible we are encouraged to set up signs, guideposts, waymarks, signposts, road markers or landmarks to remember the way that we have travelled in our lives.

Throughout the Old Testament, you see the Children of Israel doing just this:

Jacob had a dream at Bethel (Genesis 28:10-22) in which he receives an amazing promise from God. Here's part of it: -

'Your descendants will be like the dust of the earth, and you will spread out to the west and to the east, to the north and to the south. All peoples on earth will be blessed through you and your offspring. I am with you and will watch over you wherever you go, and I will bring you back to this land. I will not leave you until I have done what I have promised you.'

In response, Jacob marks the spot with a stone that he had used as a pillow the night before, and makes a vow to God: 'If God will be with me and will watch over me on this journey I am taking and will give me food to eat and clothes to wear so that I return safely to my father's household, then the Lord will be my God and this stone that I have set up as a pillar will be God's house, and of all that you give me I will give you a tenth.' He set up a memorial to mark the event, and interestingly, changed the name of the place from Luz (meaning turning away or almond tree) to Bethel (meaning house of God)!

Jacob then returns to Bethel years later (see Genesis 35) where the Lord tells him to make an altar, and he renamed the place again as El-Bethel which literally means 'God of Bethel'.

In Joshua 4:19-24, twelve stones taken from the Jordan, each representing a tribe, were set up at Gilgal. They were to remind future generations of what God had done in drying up the Jordan for His people to cross over, in just the same way that He had when he brought them through the Red Sea on dry land. The stones marked a miraculous entry into the Promised Land!

In 1 Samuel 7 we read how the Israelites turned away from idols, fasted and repented. The Philistines saw this as an opportunity to attack the Israelites whilst they were assembled. When the latter cried out to God, He thundered at the attackers, panicking and routing them and leaving the Israelites to slaughter them, bringing about a miraculous victory. Samuel's response was to set up a stone which he named Ebenezer – meaning 'Thus far the Lord has helped us'. We see two things here again – the importance of a name and the marking of God's faithfulness for all to see.

We are called to look up, look forward and look outwards for much of our walk with God – but we are never to forget the miracles He has wrought in our lives.

You may not set up a pile of stones, but you should consider how you will mark the significant breakthroughs that God has brought about in your life. You may think of different ways to do this, but one obvious way is to share your testimony. Revelation 12:11 reads 'They triumphed over him by the blood of the Lamb and by the word of their testimony.'

Don't miss out on what God has planned for your future by over-dwelling on the past!

Now Search Out the Matter

1. What are you remembering which is unhelpful? Are any adjustments required?

2. What are you being obedient in remembering? Are any adjustments required? Any praise to be given to God?

3. How will you mark God's goodness in your life so that you don't forget? What could you use instead of a pile of stones?

4. Make a list of the many good things which God has done in your life and spend time in thanksgiving. Consider adding to this list 3 or 4 times a year and setting aside time to give thanks as you review His goodness.

5. Do you ever take Communion outside of a church service? Why? Why not?

6. How do you keep the sabbath holy?

IDOLS

Which of the characteristics below would you attribute to an idol? Put a tick in the right column if you agree that it's a characteristic of an idol.

Worshipped	
Powerless	
Of no eternal value	
Consuming	
Distracting	
Short term amusement	
Addictive	
Valueless	
Man made	
Earthly	
Time consuming	
Inappropriate focus	
A substitute	
Ungodly	
Meaningless	
Toxic	
Charismatic	
Devoted to in an extreme way	
Only a representation	
Blindly adored	
Excessively admired	
Loved more than God	
Lifeless	
A mere representation	
A belief in mysticism	
Counterfeit	
Like a broken cistern	
Deceptive and seductive	

Now Search Out the Matter

1. Have you always thought the Children of Israel were foolish to create idols? Do you think idols are non-existent in modern day Western countries and cultures, or only found in Eastern countries and cultures?

2. How many of the 10 commandments relate to idols? (See Exodus 20). Where do they come in the given sequence? Why do you think that is?

3. What are the different ways the prophet defines idols in Hosea 4:12?

4. Read Jeremiah 2:11-13. Is there anything in your life which is getting more time and attention than God (i.e. an idol)? Are you seeking refreshment elsewhere? If so, which of the above characteristics can you identify regarding this idol?

5. What action must you take?

6. What or who are you placing more confidence in than God?

7. What action should you take to rectify this?

MAJESTY

As a young teenager living in South-East London, I was trainspotting one Saturday with a couple of friends at a London terminus. To our amazement that afternoon, a train pulled in just by us and Queen Elizabeth stepped off! There were not many people around, so we were able to get very close to her as she alighted from the carriage. That's the first and last time that I came close to Royalty! Her Majesty was dressed in a relatively ordinary hat and coat however we knew exactly who she was and watched her in awe as she walked by. Even in her daily attire we knew we were in the presence of someone significant. With just that single encounter, I still didn't have much of a clue as to what 'majesty' really meant.

In 1981 my company, working in telecommunications, sent me to New England with a colleague to be trained to use a very large piece of production equipment. We had flown 3,100 miles to ensure that it was all in working order before it was split into sections and sent via plane to our factory in the UK.

After time spent sightseeing in Boston over the weekend, we drove north to Danvers in Maine where we would work. I was able to watch the Royal Wedding of Prince Charles and Princess Diana from the hotel TV that Saturday. A lot of pomp and ceremony - but so many thousands of miles away from the event. This was still only a glimpse of majesty.

My colleague flew home after 10 days, but I opted to stay and visit a friend in Washington DC, via a few days in New York. It was quite a trip. I got to see the major sites in Washington escorted by my friend. Our day out included a tour of the White House. In those days you could walk up and buy tickets for the tour, then await your turn. Our excursion around the building included a few minutes in the Oval Office! Somehow this was more awe inspiring than my prior experiences, but still the President was neither there, nor was any Sovereign! All the same it gave me a flavour of the importance of the seat of power.

I had felt no fear when seeing the Queen at close quarters, and only pride at being a Brit in the USA at the time of the Royal Wedding! The Oval Office experience got me wondering about power and position and renown, but that was it. However, I was to experience something quite different and special each time that I took on a challenging mountain ascent.

I didn't get to see a mountain for real until I was 19, when I got to walk up Snowdon. Photos are great, but they don't communicate the same atmosphere and scale that you experience at the foot of, and high up on, a mountain. Through the challenge of attaining my first peak, I caught the bug, and would subsequently take days-off and summer holidays in areas of natural beauty where there were significant hills, lakes and mountains.

I still love mountains and retain vivid memories of those which I have walked and scrambled up. I couldn't always get time off work simultaneously with my friend who loved walking in the hills, so would adventure on my own. However, mountains need treating with respect and I would always stick within my capabilities. I learned to be proficient with a map and compass, and always carried waterproofs, a whistle, warm clothes and some emergency rations. I'd also let someone know which ascent I was planning that day, just in case of any issues.

I always had a sense of adventure, excitement and nerves as I set out to conquer a mountain. By then I would have carefully studied the map at length, determined the path I would take, read any relevant guidebooks and checked the weather. I was well prepared and well equipped. But I also heard too many stories of accidents and fatalities in the mountains, and I had no wish to be added to that list. The mountain was no respecter of persons. It was not going to move or change. It would look the same if I came back to it in fifty or a hundred years' time. It was silent and yet it had a real presence. I was miniscule in comparison to it. There were safe places to be on that mountain, and places to avoid. It would consume all my energy during the ascent, and often be extremely cold and exposed at its peak and on its ridges – to wind, rain, fog, mist, snow, ice, sun and more.

During hikes and scrambles on mountains I have been sunburned. I have walked in such strong winds, that I could allow my whole body to lean into the wind and still stay on my feet at an unusual angle (as its power took my full weight with ease). I have seen winds hurtling rain horizontally at speed, and then vertically up and over the ridge that I was walking on. I have walked in thick fog, and despite using all the techniques to manage in such situations, still ended up 4-5 degrees off course and not where I planned to be.

I would watch my feet over every step that I took on mountains. In order not to miss the beauty, and all the surroundings, I would take frequent breaks to be still, catch my breath and soak in the wonders all around. It would often look deceptively easy to climb! At other points on the ascent, the peak would not seem to be far away, but as the ground levelled out it would become apparent that I had been viewing a false summit.

On mountain peaks and on linking ridges I witnessed some awesome views. The mountains never moved, never made a sound, displayed amazing grandeur, threatened the life of the careless and provided new perspectives from above not observable from below.

Walking a narrow path in rain and cloud along the ridge of my favourite mountain, Suilven (in a remote area in the west of Sutherland, Scotland) at an altitude of 700 metres, I came across some small but beautiful flowers thriving despite the harsh conditions. I also encountered a pair of Ptarmigan at this altitude, completely safe and comfortable on the mountain. These birds are created to cope with cold conditions and in winter they develop thick feathers on their feet, like snowshoes! Some develop white plumage providing camouflage against the snow, typically living between 600-1200 metres above sea level!

Again, I was in awe. How could these tiny flowers and unusual birds live in these harsh conditions? If I were to stay overnight on a mountain in winter without the right equipment I could easily die.

Psalm 76:4 in the RSV is a favourite verse:

'Glorious art thou, more majestic than the everlasting mountains.'

For me, mountains represent the nearest expression of majesty and eternity on earth. A wondrous demonstration of God's creation. Places to be feared (respected); unchanging; silent yet magnificent; immovable; providing incomparable views and new perspectives; emblems of majesty.

Yet God's majesty is greater still! He too is unchanging, eternal, awesome in power, to be feared, a provider of much greater perspectives and undoubtedly majestic in a way we will only begin to grasp when we get to join Him in heaven.

It's no wonder that many significant events occurred on mountain tops throughout the Bible:

- Noah's ark came to rest on Mount Ararat

- Moses received the 10 commandments on Mount Sinai
- Elijah confronted the prophets of Baal on Mount Carmel and showcased the power of the one true God
- Abraham was brought to a place of surrender on Mount Moriah
- Jesus was transfigured, revealing His glory, on Mount Tabor (or perhaps on Mount Hermon – but definitely on a mountain!)
- Mount Calvary (Golgotha) where Jesus was crucified
- Jesus often visited and ascended the Mount of Olives where He would pray
- Mount Zion is symbolic of God's presence throughout the Bible and represents the city of the living God and the future place from where the Messiah will reign.

Now Search Out the Matter

1. Think back over your life and recall any time you experienced majesty first hand. Describe the occasion and note what aspects of majesty were evident.

2. Read the following verses and then write your own definition of majesty. Psalm 45:3; Psalm 45:4; Psalm 68:34; Psalm 93:1; Psalm 96:6; Psalm 104:1; Psalm 145:5; Isaiah 2:10; Isaiah 24:14; Hebrews 1:3

3. What contrast do you see between 2 Peter 1:16 and Isaiah 53:2? If this is not a contradiction, explain why.

4. Do a deep and thorough study on 'Zion' and then summarize what you have learned.

A CRESCENDO OF WORSHIP

Glory and
    power

(John - Revelation 1:6)

Glory,
    honour and
        power

(The 24 Elders - Revelation 4:11)

Power and
    wealth and
        wisdom and
            strength and
                honour and
                    glory and
                        praise

(Thousands of angels - Revelation 5:12)

Praise and
    glory and
        wisdom and
            thanks and
                honour and
                    power and
                      strength

(The angels, the elders, the four creatures - Revelation 7:12)

Notice how the numbers in worship increase at each step too!

Now Search Out the Matter

1. Why do you think that the scale of worship increased as revelation unfolded?

2. Consider the full list of God's character that are worshipped from all four outpourings in the 'crescendo of worship'. Does your worship today cover all of these?

3. What does it imply for your worship that the 'Lamb is worthy to receive wealth'?

4. In what way does (or should) your worship attribute honour to the Lamb?

5. Write your own 'crescendo of worship' using a favourite chapter as a springboard. (Consider using one of these passages as inspiration if you are stuck: Ephesians 1, Colossians 1, Psalm 100, Psalm 139, Psalm 145, 1 Chronicles 29:11-13)

Note: if you use this devotion in a group meeting why not read the 'crescendo of worship together out loud, starting with a whisper on the first line, and lifting the volume as each subsequent line is read.

VICTORY AMPLIFIED

In the world you have tribulation *and* distress *and* suffering, but be courageous [be confident, be undaunted, be filled with joy]; I have overcome the world. [My conquest is accomplished, My victory abiding.]

Thanks be to God, who gives us the victory [as conquerors] through our Lord Jesus Christ.

When He had disarmed the rulers and authorities [those supernatural forces of evil operating against us], He made a public example of them [exhibiting them as captives in His triumphal procession], having triumphed over them through the cross.

And He raised us up together with Him [when we believed], and seated us with Him in the heavenly *places*, [because we are] in Christ Jesus

Therefore there is now no condemnation [no guilty verdict, no punishment] for those who are in Christ Jesus [who believe in Him as personal Lord and Saviour].

Blessed *and* worthy of praise be the God and Father of our Lord Jesus Christ, who has blessed us with every spiritual blessing in the heavenly realms in Christ.

(John 16:33; 1 Corinthians 15:57; Colossians 2:15; Ephesians 2:6; Romans 8:1; Ephesians 1:3 - all from the **Amplified Bible!**)

Now Search Out the Matter

1. What does victory look like in your life?

2. Write a paragraph to describe the price paid for the victory that you have through Him.

3. How much did that victory cost you?

4. Take a moment to thank God for the victory He has secured in your life.

WISDOM

- ❖ The Key
- ❖ Wisdom
- ❖ Do You?
- ❖ What...
- ❖ Unanswered Prayer
- ❖ Seek First His Kingdom
- ❖ Stewardship

*'Wisdom is the right use of knowledge.
To know is not to be wise.
Many men know a great deal
and all the greater fools for it.
There is no fool so great a fool
as a knowing fool.
But to know how to use knowledge
is to have wisdom'*

Charles Spurgeon

THE KEY

Do you want to:
>Prolong your life for many years?
>Enjoy peace and prosperity?
>Win favour and a good name in the sight of God and man?
>Bring health to your body and nourishment to your bones?
>Have your barns overflowing and your vats brimming over with new wine?
>Know God loves you and delights in you?
>Be blessed?
>Find something more valuable than silver, gold, or rubies?
>Find something incomparable to your greatest desire?
>Enjoy long life?
>Receive riches and honour?
>Walk in pleasant ways and peace?
>Discover the tree of life?

Then:
>Don't forget my teaching.
>Keep my commands in your heart.
>Let love and faithfulness never leave you,
>bind them around your neck,
>write them on the tablet of your heart.
>Trust in the Lord with all your heart,
>and lean not on your own understanding.
>In all your ways submit to him,
>and He will make your paths straight.
>Don't be wise in your own eyes.
>Fear the Lord and shun evil.
>Honour the Lord with your wealth,
>and the first fruits of all your crops.
>Do not despise the Lord's discipline
>and do not resent his rebuke.

Proverbs 3, de-constructed

Now Search Out the Matter

1. Read the 'do you want to…' list. Pick 2-3 desires that you have from this list. Now read the counterpart – what you need to do as shown in the 'then' list. (Read Proverbs 3 itself for the 'constructed version' as this may help you make the link more easily!)

2. Now that you have the wise instruction on what to do, it's time to pray! Ask Holy Spirit if you need help actioning the solution described in Proverbs 3.

3. Commit your plan to paper and review it regularly to see how you are doing. Without action, what you have learned will simply be knowledge!

WISDOM

As a part of my business career, virtually a sideline to my main role, I used to train teams in the subject of Knowledge Management – how knowledge is acquired, captured, retained and passed on. A key part of the initial training was directed towards getting people to think about the differences between Data, Information, Knowledge and Wisdom.

Data: facts e.g. numbers, text, pictures, sounds, musical notes.

Information: data formatted for consideration, for a purpose e.g. the score for a piano piece.

Knowledge: insight gained through absorbing information and making connections, identifying lessons, linked with experience e.g. the construction of a fugue where a melody is introduced by one part and then taken up by others, all of which are interwoven to yield a harmonious delight to the ear.

Wisdom: The ability to repeatedly apply knowledge effectively e.g. Beethoven's 9th Symphony – an outcome of years and years of experience, experimentation and an expert understanding of how many instruments can be combined to create a stirring, melodious, impactful combination of sounds and textures that can delight the listener repeatedly.

There are no solid boundaries, each layer is interdependent, each layer requires the prior layers.

Information can be developed from data. It requires someone to collate and communicate data in a relevant fashion for recipients for it to become information.

Knowledge is built from a little or a lot of information and is acquired as patterns in and between that information are perceived, principles are understood, links are identified, conclusions are drawn and so on. If the outcome is then shared and learned by the recipient, they acquire bundles of knowledge.

Wisdom is not the same as having masses of knowledge, just as knowledge is not acquired simply by having lots of information and just as heaps of unformatted data do not constitute information. Wisdom requires all the layers beneath it to be explored and fully comprehended. That alone is not enough. Wisdom comes when all the above are acted upon appropriately and effective results occur, not just once, but consistently time and time again. There are no short cuts to wisdom. It is only gained through experience, the making of excellent choices and sensitive application.

The above analysis may well be incomplete, but I hope at the very least, it has got you thinking. Is there a connection between this kind of 'human' wisdom and Biblical wisdom? You can read Bible verses (data) in organised chapters and read commentaries (information) and cross-reference texts, meditate on and memorize scripture, explore theology and spend time in Bible study (knowledge). However, I believe wisdom only occurs when you know, understand and repeatedly apply Biblical truth, act in obedience, step out in faith and make Spirit-filled decisions.

Foolishness is having all the data, information and knowledge, but then doing the wrong thing, making the wrong choices and not being willing to be corrected. Here are God's thoughts on the matter in 1 Corinthians 3:19:

> "For the wisdom of this world is foolishness in God's sight. As it is written: 'He catches the wise in their craftiness'"

Now Search Out the Matter

1. Time to go deeper! There are over 400 instances of the word 'wisdom' in the Bible. That makes for a huge study, so focus on the 50 instances that are found in the book of Proverbs.

2. Review each of the 50 verses and make notes about what they teach you regarding wisdom. You can use the following questions to aid your study:

    a. What is wisdom useful for?
    b. How is wisdom acquired?
    c. What or who is the source of wisdom?
    d. Where should/does wisdom reside?
    e. What impact does wisdom have on the owner?
    f. How should wisdom be regarded?
    g. How is wisdom described – directly or indirectly? What is it likened to?
    h. How valuable is wisdom?
    i. What rewards does wisdom bring?
    j. What stems from wisdom?
    k. How is wisdom linked to discernment?
    l. Is wisdom learned, acquired or given?

DO YOU?

Do you think you won't be healed because you are unworthy?
*I don't heal anyone based on their self-worth.
I heal them based on my Son's sacrifice and their worth in my eyes.*

Do you think you won't receive my gifts because you lack spirituality?
*I don't give my gifts based on your spirituality.
I give them out of the abundance of my heart and as you surrender.*

Do you carry your shame with you every day because you believe you are unforgivable?
*I don't free you from shame based on your self-evaluation.
I free you from shame because of my Son's shed blood.*

Do you aim to secure my favour because you think you can earn it?
*I don't bestow my favour on you based on your actions.
I pour favour out on you as you trust and obey and because I am your Father.*

Do you worship me because you think you should?
*I don't receive your worship based on your thoughts or 'oughts'.
I receive your worship when you heart responds in genuine love for me and in awe of my character.*

Do you base your security on what you have?
*I don't value you by what you have accumulated.
I value you by the price Jesus paid.*

Do you think that long prayers will win me over?
*The length of your prayers is irrelevant to me.
I look only at the size of your heart and the measure of faith that I discover.*

Now Search Out the Matter

1. Are there lies and messages that reverberate in your head which are not Biblical, and which hold you back from enjoying an abundant life?

2. If so, find their Biblical antidotes and write down these words of truth. You might want to put them somewhere prominent in your home so you can read them often. Memorize the relevant verses and rehearse them out loud regularly. Be wise!

WHAT...

...is like a gold earring or an ornament of fine gold?

...is better than hidden love?

...causes both horse and chariot to lie still?

...is oil on your head?

...causes the wise to love you?

...impresses a discerning person?

...will have favour in the end?

...is better than listening to the song of fools?

...dried up the Red Sea?

...comes with flames of fire?

...quietened and stilled the wind and waves?

...heals fevers?

...casts out demons?

...must not be used harshly with an older man?

...is one of the things scripture is profitable for?

...should be done with encouragement and all authority?

...is a sign of love?

Still stuck?

Then check out the following verses in the NIV:

Proverbs 25:12; Proverbs 27:5; Psalm 76:6; Psalm 141:5; Proverbs 9:8; Proverbs 17:10; Proverbs 28:23; Ecclesiastes 7:5; Isaiah 50:2; Isaiah 66:15; Mark 4:39; Luke 4:39; Luke 4:41; 1 Timothy 5:1; 2 Timothy 3:16; Titus 2:15; Revelation 3:19

Now Search Out the Matter

---

1. Now re-read the previous page and include the word you have discovered with each phrase.

2. Surprised by anything?

3. Touched by anything?

4. What would be wise to change in your life, in your reactions?

5. Write a paragraph defining wisdom based on the above verses.

UNANSWERED PRAYER

'Unanswered prayer' is a widely used expression. It could just be me, but I believe in many cases when we say this, we mean 'God didn't do what I wanted!' That aside, does God *always* answer prayer? If not, I'd like to understand why not. Here are a few things which might explain why (feel free to agree or disagree with any of these, but ensure you have your own view on this topic!!!):

- *I wasn't listening when He spoke*
- *He's already answered, but I didn't like the answer*
- *The answer's already in His Word*
- *I'm not ready to receive the answer yet*
- *What I've asked for may not be the best for me*
- *I asked something outside of His will*
- *He wants to see if I'll be faithful and trust Him if He's silent*
- *I already have the God-given capacity to derive the answer*
- *What I want to know is a divine mystery*
- *I don't need to know the answer*
- *He simply wants me to trust in His Sovereignty*
- *I didn't obey the last time around*
- *He's developing my patience*
- *He wants me to figure this one out*
- *It's His timing not mine*

Now Search Out the Matter

So – did you agree with any or each of the above rationales as to why your prayers were unanswered?

1. List three times when you felt God didn't answer your prayers.

2. Could any of the above possible rationales be the reason? If so, which one (or more) applied in your situation?

3. Still stuck? Ask God to show you!!

4. Read Psalm 77:
    - Does the writer believe that God has answered his prayer?
    - What is the turning point?
    - What is his approach thereafter?

SEEK FIRST HIS KINGDOM

Once we grasp the truth that what we have been given is not ours, but rather what we have been blessed with, it changes how we perceive everything that He has entrusted to us. If we have plenty, then God has enriched us for a reason, and He expects us to invest and sow it wisely in His Kingdom as He leads. If we have little, it may require very practical faith trusting in Jehovah Jireh – God our provider!

I have lived in both states. Paul describes this well in Philippians 4:11-13 NLT, 'Not that I was ever in need, for I have learned how to be content with whatever I have. I know how to live on almost nothing or with everything. I have learned the secret of living in every situation, whether it is with a full stomach or empty, with plenty or little. For I can do everything through Christ, who gives me strength.'

As a child, one of five, there were times when my parents were running very low on cash, despite my dad working several jobs. I would wear hand-me-down clothes, or wear others which once fitted me, but I had then outgrown. There was not always enough money to replace them.

My brother and I went to university at the same time which meant that the Government grant for one student had to be split between us. In my first year, once I had paid for full board and lodging for a term, I had £14 left for anything else, like books, coffee, etc. To put this in context, a return train ticket home cost over £5 at that time. To join a Christian Conference in Germany in the Easter of my final year, I had to sell my radio-cassette player to a friend to raise enough cash to pay for the conference and travel. I had a job in my student holidays and had saved carefully, so that I could buy this. It was my pride and joy for three years, but now I needed the cash to pay for the Conference.

At the end of that summer, I began work. In the first week I went to the Personnel Department to ask for my first pay packet to be issued early, or I could not afford to travel to work, buy food or even a quilt, cover and sheets. A friend also made me a short-term loan.

During the seven years working for this company, I had been promoted 4 times and was on a great trajectory within the business. In the latter years I had the privilege of producing annual manufacturing plans and 10-year strategic plans for the company. This gave me the chance to work with senior managers and directors. However, I felt God was calling me to work as a Regional Administrator for The Navigators (a parachurch organisation working with students). When I told my boss I would be leaving and what I was going to do, he arranged for me to spend time with our director. After I had explained my intentions to this senior guy and what I was planning, he indicated that, if I stayed, I would probably become a director down the road. I think he was bothered that I was being seduced by some strange religious sect and so, having failed to persuade me to change my mind, he set up an appointment with the Group Personnel Director to see if he could talk some sense into me! I got a good hearing and no pressure to alter course. I really respected the time they spent and the concern they showed in ensuring that I was being wise.

This sudden career change also bothered my parents – they didn't articulate this, but I could tell they were worried. After all, they'd invested much to give me an excellent education and though they were Christians, they were naturally anxious that I fully understood what I was getting into. However, as always, they supported me.

The new role was to be part-time, so I would rapidly need to find another part-time job. The first was unpaid, so I needed the second to help fund living costs. Friends and family also committed to monthly financial support. I was to be a 'tentmaker' like the apostle Paul (see Acts 18:1-4, Acts 20:33-35, Philippians 4:14-16) – working to earn money alongside serving those evangelising and ministering to students.

I studied Ergonomics (or Human Factors as the Americans know it) for my degree. A few of my lecturers, including a Professor and an Industrial Ergonomist (who also happened to be a Christian) had set up a research and consultancy centre (Human Sciences and Advanced Technology) within the University some years before. I discovered a role that they were recruiting for – just at the right time – the interviews taking place before I left my full-time job. There were several candidates, and each had to rotate through 8 or 9 fifteen-minute interviews with members of staff, each assessing a different aspect.

I recall very clearly praying that if this whole move away from my current salaried career was right, seeking first His Kingdom, that God would honour it with success in these interviews. I also chose to add a 'Gideon's fleece'. I prayed that if this was God's will for me, then every single interviewer would have said 'yes' to my recruitment. The thing that I never thought about was – how would I know if this was the case???

A few days later I got a call at work. It was the Executive Director from HUSAT (the Christian chap) to say that I had succeeded in attaining the role, and by the way, 'it was a unanimous decision, with everyone you saw saying 'yes''.

Through the next 4-5 years I never lacked the cash to pay my mortgage, bills or my food. I also got married during this time, though soon after my wife was made redundant. Close friends had given me the money to buy an engagement ring for my fiancée, and my parents chipped in on the wedding costs. Katie's ancient car had to be scrapped, and mine needed a lot to keep it on the road, but we managed to buy a cheap and cheerful Citroën Dyane.

Five years further on I moved back into a business environment, securing a role with a blue-chip company. I started on a salary 60% higher than my previous role despite the unusual career diversion I had taken seeking His kingdom! Matthew 6:33 was, and continues to be, true in my life:

'But seek first his kingdom and his righteousness, and all these things will be given to you as well.'

Over the next 30 years, I worked in finance for this global company and God kept blessing me, eventually raising me into a senior treasury position even though I don't have a single finance qualification! Our unfailing and constant God kept His side of this conditional promise!

Now Search Out the Matter

1. The Greek word for 'seek' in Matthew 6:33 is zéteó (ζητέω) which means to search, desire, require, aim at, strive after and 'to seek in order to find'. Does this describe the approach to your relationship with God and His Word?

2. Ask Holy Spirit to show you any area of your life where you are anxious about daily issues and where you could choose to apply the truth of this verse?

3. What will you change? Write it down and share this with a friend so they can help you to be accountable.

4. The same Greek word is found in Matthew 7:7. Can you testify to the truth of this verse?

5. In John 1:38, Jesus asks two of John's disciples 'What do you want?' or 'What do you seek?'. Imagine Jesus asking you that question right now – what would your answer be?

STEWARDSHIP

For the last third of my career, I was a Corporate Treasurer for a private company where my responsibilities ranged across Europe, the Middle East, Africa and India, and embraced half a dozen global functions.

When most people hear the word 'Treasurer' they probably think of the person who collects and accounts for the cash at their club, charity or church. This function in the business world is much the same. I used to define it this way when explaining 'Treasury' to those across our business:

'Ensuring the right amount of cash is available, in the right currency, at the right price, in the right place, at the right time, for the right purpose.'

This may as well be called 'Cash Logistics' - logistics is all about having the right product, at the right price, in the right place, at the right time for the right purpose. Military logistics follows the same line of thinking: to fight a battle, you need the right troops, in the right place, with the right armaments, and sufficient fuel and ordnance, at the right time, to face the enemy.

My treasury team, on behalf of our global business, received cash from our customers, paid our suppliers, and settled the cash transactions between our factories and markets. During my time in role, we handled cashflows of many, many billions of dollars.

At no point did I own any of this cash, nor did our factories or market offices. It was a family owned, private company, and the family were the shareholders. Our task was to gather the cash together in one place, see that it was invested or used according to the requirements of our owners – to build new factories, to add new manufacturing equipment, to pay for raw materials and packaging, to build stock, to pay our workforce, to float new initiatives, to make acquisitions, to pay down debt, to pay dividends to our owners, and more. It was not our cash, and not ours to decide what to use it for.

We were highly accountable to record every cent and ensure it was well looked after once our businesses had generated it, to invest it wisely, but always have enough available cash to meet daily needs.

Simply put, a steward is a person who manages someone else's affairs. In every sense of the word, we were stewards for the family who owned this amazing global business.

To give an insight into what a Christian steward is, let's start with comparing it to the Corporate Treasury role.

Treasury Steward	**Christian Steward**
Manages someone else's cash	Manages God's cash
Doesn't own the cash	Doesn't own the cash
Entrusted with much	Entrusted with much
Is accountable to owners / shareholders	Is accountable to God
Is financially rewarded	Is richly rewarded
Moves cash as instructed by owners for multiple purposes	Tithes, gives and sows according to God's direction
Invests wisely for the owners/shareholders	Invests wisely for the body of Christ
Invests for the short and long term	Invests for eternity
Is a signatory on company bank accounts	Is a signatory on God's bank accounts

For many decades now I have looked at giving in a new way. I came to realise that giving was all about moving cash from one of God's accounts to another of *His* accounts - rather than from one of *my* accounts to that of another person in need.

Everything we have comes from Him. James 1:17 reminds us that 'Every good and perfect gift is from above, coming down from the Father of the heavenly lights, who does not change like shifting shadows.'

Thus, everything we have, whether it be health, money, family, skills, possessions – all these come from Him. As such they belong to Him, but He chooses to entrust these into our care and expects us to use them for His Kingdom.

Our focus should be very clear from Matthew 6:33, 'Seek first his kingdom and his righteousness, and all these things will be given to you as well.' The 'all these things' cover our daily basic needs – a home, clothes, food and drink.

2 Peter 1:3 in the ESV reads, 'His divine power has granted to us all things that pertain to life and godliness, through the knowledge of him who called us to his own glory and excellence.' I've spent a lot of time chewing this verse over and just **CANNOT** think of anything that I need which falls outside of 'all things that pertain to life' or 'all things which pertain to godliness'. I have everything I need from Him! So, it all belongs to Him, comes from Him and all I can do is give back to God what He has given to me! Yet he chooses us to steward all of that on His behalf! It's amazing!

We are called to steward everything which God gives us: our bodies, our time, our relationships, our energy, our money, our possessions, our skills and abilities, our love, and much more.

Now Search Out the Matter

1. Read Genesis 41:41-57. In what ways was Joseph a good steward? What stewardship principles can you identify?

2. Read Daniel 2:48-49 and 6:4. In what ways was Daniel a good steward, and how was he rewarded?

3. Read 2 Kings 18:1-8 and 2 Chronicles 31:20-21. Consider the way in which Hezekiah is described. In what ways do you consider he was a good steward?

4. Read Matthew 25:14-30. List the principles of good stewardship taught by Jesus.

5. Would you say that you are a wise steward?

FEAR

- Victory Means Victory
- Fear
- Fear Of The Lord
- Fear Without God
- Fear Not
- True Fear Of The Lord
- Mystery

*'We must fear God out of love,
not love Him out of fear'*

Saint Francis de Sales

VICTORY MEANS VICTORY

The ultimate victory in Christ is found in salvation and forgiveness of sins offered to all who believe in Him. Through faith in Jesus, we are reconciled with God and receive eternal life.

In Christ, we have the power to overcome sin and temptation. Through the indwelling of the Holy Spirit, we are empowered to resist the lure of sinful desires and live a life that is pleasing to God.

Victory in Christ involves breaking free from spiritual, emotional, and mental bondage. It includes deliverance from unhealthy patterns, addictions, and any form of oppression through the power of Christ.

Victory in Christ results in the transformation of one's character. We are called to live in righteousness and imitate the character of Christ. Through the process of sanctification, the Holy Spirit works in our lives to produce the fruit of the Spirit, such as love, joy, peace, patience, kindness, goodness, faithfulness, gentleness, and self-control.

In Christ, we can find victory over fear and anxiety. We can take comfort in His promises and trust in His faithfulness, knowing that He is with us in every circumstance.

We are engaged in spiritual warfare, but in Christ, we have the victory. By putting on the armour of God, we can overcome the schemes of the enemy and stand firm in our faith.

Ephesians 6:12 reminds us: 'For our struggle is not against flesh and blood, but against the rulers, against the authorities, against the powers of this dark world and against the spiritual forces of evil in the heavenly realms.' Yet we are still victors!

Victory in Christ brings hope and assurance of a future glory. During trials and tribulations, we can find comfort in the knowledge that we are secure in Christ and that He has overcome the world.

Victory in Christ is not about an absence of challenges or hardships, but rather a steadfast trust in the power and love of Jesus Christ, knowing that He has conquered sin and death and that nothing can separate believers from His love.

Now Search Out the Matter

1. Read 2 Chronicles 20 and make a note of the keys to unlocking victory for Jehoshophat.

2. Ask Holy Spirit to show you an area of your life in which you need victory.

3. Now find someone you really trust and ask them to pray with you to gain victory in this area of your life.

FEAR

Fear defies all that I am.
It interferes with understanding everything that I have
prepared for you.
It prevents joy and peace from reaching you.
It deceives you into believing many lies.
It smothers your ability to think,
to listen and to fellowship with me.
It causes grace to be blocked off.
It stunts your growth.
It focuses your mind on what might happen,
not on what I can do,
or on what I have promised you.

I am the all-mighty one!
No-one compares with me.
You cannot imagine the power that I have,
nor my majesty -
yet you are my children, loved and accepted.
These two elements must be kept in balance -
to fully perceive who I am, and who you are.

Those who are in me have nothing to fear.
Those without me are lost.

Stop defending all the things you cling to.
Let go of all that is not in line with my word,
and you will discover great freedom.

Be bold.
Have courage.
Trust my word and my leading,
and you will find a way through to peace and fulfilment,
that will be far greater than all that you have been seeking, or
that you have found in worldly things.

Don't hesitate to obey.
Start now and enjoy the freedom I have for you.
Never go back.
Meditate on my word.
Give thanks for all I have done.
Claim my promises.
Receive my peace.
Clear your mind and be still.
Remember I will not fail you.

My words are truth -
truth sets you free.
Listen for my guidance, not to the lies of the enemy.
Understanding who I am, and soaking in my Word
gives you the foundation from which to reject all fear and lies.
It gives you the foundation to build with truth –
adding truth to truth to truth.
Truth brings clarity and freedom.

Grow strong in knowing me,
in trusting me
and the deceptions of the enemy will be exposed.
Lose sight of me,
and you will soon feel defeated,
and blinded from the truth.
Renew your mind.
This is the key.

I want you to know my child that I am always here for you.
Never think that you cannot approach me.
I am the Almighty, however,
Jesus' blood has opened direct access –
right into my presence!
Without fear!
The way has been cleared.

Your days may seem to be exhausting and heavy,

but I remain unchanging,
as does my love and my desire for you and your family.
You are central to my thoughts, and I love you all dearly.
Do not allow lies to deceive you.
I will carry you through the storm.
We will come out the other side walking together,
safe on the rock.

I want to walk with you always and talk with you,
and show you so much more of my love,
and of my Kingdom.

For now, simply trust in me.
This is the place of peace.
This is the place of hope.
This is the place of joy.
This is where I want you to come, rest and remain.

As long as we walk together,
nothing can touch you or yours.
You will be safe in my company.
So, rest now, and enjoy me!

Keep letting go,
and you will find a new path to yet more peace.

There is a lie which underlies all fear….

…that my words will not be fulfilled.

As soon as that thought enters your heart,
or anything which is not of me enters your mind,
fear floods your soul.
But if you open your heart to my words,
and actively stand on their truth,
and declare and claim them in your life,
you can withstand and refute the lie.

And my Spirit will lead you into all truth,
into my perfect love,
where there is no fear.

Now Search Out the Matter

---

1. Ask Holy Spirit to show you any fears, anxieties, or insecurities which you are still carrying.

2. Pray that you would be overwhelmed by His perfect love. Declare His love and freedom immediately when fear raises its head in your life. Repeat until you are free.

FEAR OF THE LORD

'A religious expression conveying either devotional piety or the dread of punishment'. The term 'Lord' in this context refers to Yahweh.

Why should anyone be in 'fear' of the Lord, as in 'terrified' of Him? Let's start with those who refuse to accept Him, who refuse to believe in Him, who refuse to accept His sacrifice – they should be mightily afraid:

Reference	Punishment
Romans 6:23	Death
Psalm 145:20	Destruction
Matthew 25:46	Eternal punishment
Galatians 6:7	Reaping what has been sown
Romans 5:12	What is due, death
John 3:36	God's wrath
Romans 2:6-10	Tribulation and distress
Revelation 20:15	Lake of fire
John 5:29	Resurrection of judgement
Matthew 25:41	Eternal fire
Revelation 20:10	Torment day and night forever
John 3:3	Never seeing the kingdom of God

Whilst none of us may wish to become a 'hellfire and damnation' preacher, we should not shy away from the truth facing those who choose not to receive forgiveness and enter the kingdom. For them, the most terrible of punishments is, in my mind, to be eternally in a place where God is not. The blood of Jesus does not protect them from God's wrath there.

Now Search Out the Matter

1. Do you believe your non-Christian friends should be aware of their fate if they do not receive Jesus as their Saviour?

2. Note down the name of a close friend who does not know the Lord and with whom you have not shared the Gospel yet. If you were out walking with them and they stepped out into the road in front of a car, what would you do?

3. Pray for them daily if you don't already.

4. Ask Holy Spirit for an opportunity to share the good news with them.

5. When that opportunity arises, ask them where they are going when they die. Explain what the good news is, and what the bad news is, depending on what they decide.

FEAR WITHOUT GOD

Many years ago, my first business trip to Australia spanned several weeks, thus giving me the opportunity to explore in my free time, especially over the weekend.

Whilst in Sydney, I decided to take a ferry from Darling Harbour across to Taronga zoo. Whilst I enjoyed zoos as a child, I grew to dislike them as an adult because of the unnatural captivity, confining the animals and stealing their freedom. However, I was keen to see animals that were not native to my home country, some of which are only found in Australia.

Having disembarked from the ferry, I spent several hours at the zoo, but I have just one memory remaining today – it has never left me, because of the lasting impression that it made!

I was walking along a pathway in the midday sun and noticed what looked like a prison window in a thickset concrete wall. The bars were tubular and appeared very strong, set deep into the concrete. The aperture was not that large, and in contrast to the dazzling sunlight that I was bathed in, the view through this window from a distance was very dark. Not knowing what to expect, I approached and peered in. I couldn't see anything. As I continued to investigate the gloom, in anticipation of seeing whatever lay within, I got the fright of my life.

My presence, or my scent, or the sound of my approach, or my silhouette shutting out what little light penetrated this 'cell', had clearly disturbed its incumbent. What followed terrified me. It was the rear of the lions' den. The beast must have spun round, leapt at the window and released the loudest roar that I have ever heard. My heart pounded so hard, and so fast. It was a moment of absolute terror – the sudden surprise and sheer volume of its roar put my body into shock! This roaring lion, king of the jungle, was just a few feet away when it let rip! What's more, I still couldn't see it – but, my goodness, I knew exactly what it was, and how close it must have been at that very moment!

Of course, I was completely safe! I was protected by what lay between us. Although it was quite some time before my resting heartbeat returned. And the experience from decades ago remains very vivid in my memory to this day.

Until the point I came to Christ in repentance, I fully deserved the full weight of a holy God's justice and anger towards my sin. At the instant of salvation, I received eternal protection from God's wrath, because the blood of the Lamb cleared my debt. Jesus stood between me and certain death – just as a solid wall and a steel barred window protected me from being ripped to pieces by a ferocious roaring lion! Just as I was terrified by that lion's roar, so too, it is appropriate that I was terrified of God's wrath before I was saved. And in the same way that I retain a vivid memory of my fear of that lion, so too, it is only right that I should maintain my fear of the Lord, even though I have been completely released from the penalty of my actions and ignorance.

Now Search Out the Matter

1. Does the 'fear of the Lord' mean you should live in everyday terror of Him?

2. How does the way you live your life demonstrate a healthy fear of the Lord?

3. Are there any ways in which you are living that are not yet aligned with a true fear of the Lord? Ask Holy Spirit to show you. When He brings some area of your life to mind which is not yet fully yielded, take time right now to repent and seek His help.

4. Make a series of regular diary notes to review anything Holy Spirit reveals, as this may be the start of a new journey into Christlikeness – something you may need to keep reviewing and where your mind still needs regularly renewing!

FEAR NOT

The English language is notorious for utilising the same word for multiple meanings. It must be a nightmare at times for the foreigner as they attempt to learn the language. Take the word 'leave', for example: it can mean abandon, resign, depart, remain, bequeath, permission, holiday, etc. Consider the word 'right': it can mean correct, direct, true, fitting, genuine, truly judged, accurate, justifiable, equitable, commendable, side, etc. From these examples we see that context is always the vital clue to accurate understanding of a word.

When we think of 'fear', what comes to mind? According to the Chambers Dictionary, there are two major meanings in English. Firstly, a painful emotion excited by danger; apprehension of danger or pain; alarm, solicitude, anxiety. Secondly it may mean reverence, awe, piety towards God, veneration.

So which type of fear does the Bible speak of? The Lexham Bible Dictionary sums it up succinctly, 'A religious expression conveying either devotional piety or the dread of punishment.'

I believe the 'fear of the Lord' encompasses both elements. John Newton expresses this truth so beautifully and succinctly in his well-known hymn, 'Amazing Grace':

'Twas grace that taught my heart to fear,
And grace my fears relieved

Let's explore this distinction further.

The Bible includes many occasions where a person is told 'Do not fear', 'Don't be afraid'.

In the Old Testament it was said to Abraham, Hagar, Moses, the children of Israel (many times), Joshua, Gideon, Ruth, the widow at Zarephath, Solomon, Jehoshaphat, Ahaz, Jeremiah, Ezekiel, and Daniel.

In the New Testament it was said to Joseph, Zechariah, Mary, the shepherds, the twelve disciples, Jairus and his household, Simon, Paul, and John.

We are certainly in good company! Whilst it is true that our bodies are wired to react when our lives are threatened by circumstances (like my lion encounter), we are not to live in a state of fear. In fact, fear is probably the most utilised tool of the enemy in his attempt to throw us off our journey to Christlikeness. Therefore, we need to be ready for his attacks. Arming yourself with scripture is a good place to start!

The verses that follow are a condensed reminder of all that we have and are in Christ. There is much more in the scriptures – this is just a short compilation to get you started as you deny fear a place in your heart.

> *'For I am convinced that neither death nor life, neither angels nor demons, neither the present nor the future, nor any powers, height nor depth, nor anything else in all creation, will be able to separate us from the love of God that is in Christ Jesus our Lord.'*
>
> Romans 8:38-39

> *'I will ask the Father, and he will give you another advocate to help you and be with you for ever – the Spirit of truth.'*
>
> John 14:16-17

> *'So do not fear, for I am with you; do not be dismayed, for I am your God. I will strengthen you and help you; I will uphold you with my righteous right hand.'*
>
> Isaiah 41:10

'For I am the LORD your God who takes hold of your right hand and says to you, 'Do not fear; I will help you'.'

Isaiah 41:13

'Do not be anxious about anything, but in every situation, by prayer and petition, with thanksgiving, present your requests to God. And the peace of God, which transcends all understanding, will guard your hearts and your minds in Christ Jesus.'

Philippians 4: 6-7

'Be strong and courageous. Do not be afraid or terrified because of them, for the LORD your God goes with you; he will never leave you nor forsake you.'

Deuteronomy 31:6

Now Search Out the Matter

1. Write a letter to a friend (or yourself), based on the above passages, explaining why they should not be afraid.

2. Select one of the Old Testament individuals to whom the words 'Fear not' were spoken. What followed in their life that might explain why God spoke this to them?

3. Repeat the above for one of the New Testament characters to whom the same words were spoken.

4. What situations in life cause you to be afraid? What steps can you take to overcome your fear? Get together with someone you are comfortable with and pray together for freedom from fear.

TRUE FEAR OF THE LORD

What does the correct fear of the Lord look like? Let's see what scripture has to say:

Fear of the Lord should cause you to…

> Trust in Him
> Walk in obedience to Him
> Love Him
> Serve Him with all your heart and all your soul
> Judge carefully
> Praise Him
> Revere Him
> Avoid evil
> Delight in Him

Fear of the Lord is…

> Learned
> The beginning of wisdom
> The beginning of knowledge
> A rich store of salvation, wisdom, and knowledge
> Humility
> Pure
> Enduring forever
> A fountain of life
> Better than wealth with turmoil
> To honour His name
> Zion's treasure

How do you get started in understanding true fear?

What is the impact of true fear of the Lord?

Proverbs 9:10
'**The fear of the LORD** is the beginning of wisdom,
and knowledge of the Holy One is understanding.'

Proverbs 1:7
'**The fear of the LORD** is the beginning of knowledge,
but fools despise wisdom and instruction.'

Proverbs 3:7
'Do not be wise in your own eyes;
Fear the Lord and shun evil.'

Deuteronomy 10:12-13
'And now, Israel, what does the LORD your God ask of you but to **fear the LORD your God**, to walk in obedience to him, to love him, to serve the LORD your God with all your heart and with all your soul, and to observe the LORD's commands and decrees that I am giving you today for your own good?'

James 1:5-6
'If any of you lacks **wisdom**, you should **ask God**, who gives generously to all without finding fault, and it will be given to you. But when you ask, **you must believe** and not doubt, because the one who doubts is like a wave of the sea, blown and tossed by the wind.'

*All words in **bold** are my emphasis*

Now Search Out the Matter

1. Time to get your thinking cap on! Write your own definition of 'fear of the Lord'. Use whatever materials you need as input, but ensure you believe in your written definition.

2. Who or what do you live in fear of? Why?

3. Fear of the Lord should cause you to live in ways that the Bible indicates - as we have just seen. Ask Holy Spirit to show you if there is any way in which an aspect of the fear of the Lord is missing. For example, is there an area in your life of disobedience which needs repentance? Is there an area of your life where you feel unable to 'delight in Him'? Review the list and listen for what the Lord wants to help you with.

MYSTERY

When my wife Katie was very ill, we visited a 'healing room' in London regularly. On one occasion as we were waiting for her to be prayed for, a young woman came across the room and asked if she could pray for my wife and draw a picture using her prophetic art gift. Katie agreed, and whilst the team prayed for her healing, this young lady sat in the waiting room, prayed, then drew a simple picture which she gave my wife at the end of our time there. It was a child-like colour drawing and was an exact picture of our lounge, with windows correctly placed, accurately coloured curtains and sofa with a display shelf above it. She sensed God had shown her the 'special place' where Katie spent regular time with God and would continue to do so. At that point we had not encountered the 'prophetic art' gift, and we were both stunned at the accuracy of the drawing and the precise identification of Katie's 'special place' where she spent intimate hours with God in prayer and listening.

During the 18 months that I spent writing this book, Holy Spirit indicated many topics that I had not considered before and needed to look at more closely. Mystery was one of these. As I prayed and wrote what I heard, I soon learned where mystery was likely to be revealed:

> 'There are mysteries that are currently hidden from you,
> which I long to reveal to you,
> when you spend time in your special place with me.
>
> But know this,
> there are also mysteries which will not be revealed –
> which require you to stay in faith and
> depend on my unfailing character.
>
> I will reveal everything that you need to know,

as and when you need to know it.
Nothing is withheld from you that you need.
I want you to continue to trust in me
during the most difficult and unusual circumstances,
because my heart for you is to develop you
into the likeness of my Son - into His fullness.

And that requires faith, in which I always delight.
I take great pleasure when you step forward in faith.
Don't lose time worrying over things which are not yet
revealed.
However, know this –
that there are things which I want to explain
to help you understand.

In the past season, there have been mysteries,
things you have not understood,
things I've not revealed to you.
There is a time coming soon,
when I'll open your eyes to see in ways like never before.

I long to show you more of Myself!
I'm going to take you to a new place!
To a new level!
Higher with me!

I'm going to show you,
my goodness,
my abundance,
my faithfulness,
because you have honoured me,
because you have been faithful.

I delight in your worship and our time together.
Don't trade that special time for anything else.
There is much in front of you which is of limited and short-
term value.

Draw close to me as Mary did.
Sit at my feet and listen.
It's in this place of rest,
where you focus on me,
that I will reveal what you need to know.
I will reveal to you what has been hidden.
I will show you new and great things.

I am your Sovereign God!'

Now Search Out the Matter

1. Look up the definition of the word 'mystery' in one or more dictionaries.

2. Look up the following verses and see what you can learn about divine mystery:
   a. Job 11:7
   b. Jeremiah 33:3
   c. Daniel 2:28-30, 47
   d. Acts 1:6-7
   e. Romans 11:25
   f. Romans 16:25
   g. 1 Corinthians 2:7
   h. 1 Corinthians 4:1
   i. 1 Corinthians 13:2
   j. Ephesians 1:9
   k. Ephesians 3:3-9
   l. Ephesians 5:32
   m. 1 Timothy 3:16
   n. Revelation 10:7

3. See if you can find further verses which talk about mystery.

4. Is everything revealed? What are some important mysteries described in these verses? Now write your own definition of divine mystery.

HEART

- ❖ Choose Well
- ❖ Always Or Sometimes
- ❖ Pray For Your Heart
- ❖ My Heart's State
- ❖ A Prayer For My Heart
- ❖ Pray This For Your Heart
- ❖ My Heart's Response

'Who is pure of heart?
Only those who have surrendered their
hearts completely to Jesus that He may
reign in them alone.'

Dietrich Bonhoeffer

CHOOSE WELL

HE OFFERS THIS	INSTEAD OF	
A crown of beauty	Ashes	*Isaiah 61:3*
Oil of joy	Mourning	*Isaiah 61:3*
Garment of praise	Spirit of despair	*Isaiah 61:3*
Double portion	Shame	*Isaiah 61:7*
An inheritance	Disgrace	*Isaiah 61:7*
Gladness	Mourning	*Jeremiah 31:13*
Comfort and joy	Sorrow	*Jeremiah 31:13*
Instruction	Silver	*Proverbs 8:10*
Knowledge	Choice gold	*Proverbs 8:10*
Juniper	Thorn-bush	*Isaiah 55:13*
Myrtle	Briers	*Isaiah 55:13*
Friendship	Servanthood	*John 15:15*
More grace	Grace given	*John 1:16*
Forgiveness	Our sin	*Matthew 26:28*

BE THIS	INSTEAD OF BEING	
A servant	Great	*Matthew 20:26*
A correct judge of others	A judge based on appearances	*John 7:24*
Forgiving	Aggrieved	*2 Corinthians 2:5-7*
A speaker of truth in love	Tossed to-and-fro	*Ephesians 4:14-15*
Filled with the Spirit	Drunk on wine	*Ephesians 5:18*
An instructor of your children	Exasperating to them	*Ephesians 6:4*
A seeker of His will	Fixed on your plan	*James 4:13-15*

Now Search Out the Matter

1. Pick one or more of the lines from the top table on the previous page that caught your eye. Read the related text (and its surrounding verses). Consider to what extent you have received what God offers, and to what extent you are holding on to what He wants to replace.

2. Now do the same with the second table. Does anything in the right column describe you in part or in full, and what steps do you need to take to 'be fully' who God wants you to be (as in the first column)?

3. What is the imagery being used in Isaiah 55:13? Why Juniper and myrtle versus thorn-bush and brier? What do they each represent?

ALWAYS OR SOMETIMES?

Which is the closest description of how you think and live?

Rejoice in the Lord **sometimes**. I will say it again: rejoice! Your Life Version???	**OR**	**Philippians 4:4** Rejoice in the Lord **always**. I will say it again: rejoice! New International Version
...speaking to one another with psalms, hymns, and songs from the Spirit. Sing and make music from your heart to the Lord, **sometimes** giving thanks to God the Father for everything, in the name of our Lord Jesus Christ. Your Life Version???	**OR**	**Ephesians 5:19-20** ...speaking to one another with psalms, hymns, and songs from the Spirit. Sing and make music from your heart to the Lord, **always** giving thanks to God the Father for everything, in the name of our Lord Jesus Christ. New International Version
But thanks be to God, who **sometimes** leads us as captives in Christ's triumphal procession and uses us to spread the aroma of the knowledge of him everywhere. Your Life Version???	**OR**	**2 Corinthians 2:14** But thanks be to God, who **always** leads us as captives in Christ's triumphal procession and uses us to spread the aroma of the knowledge of him everywhere. New International Version

I'm always amazed just how few words the Bible uses to describe so very much. The gospels combined contain less than 65,000 words. So much is said in so few words – and I am absolutely convinced that every single word matters. Some words have a variety of meanings or require careful interpretation, whilst others are black and white every time – like 'always' – it always means always!

Now Search Out the Matter

---

1. Now have some fun exploring…
   Which words in the following pairs are used more than the other in the New Testament?
   Have a guess first then search it out!

Centurion	*or*	Repentance
Temple	*or*	Kingdom
Jesus	*or*	Christ
Paul	*or*	Peter
Righteousness	*or*	Pharisee

2. How often is the word 'power' used in the book of Acts? List everyone who is said to have power. What did you learn?

3. Find New Testament verses which include the word 'faith' and experiment by replacing it with 'belief'. How is the significance of the original word amplified when compared to its replacement?

PRAY FOR YOUR HEART

As a result of a detailed study, I discovered over 700 verses that speak about the heart. I decided to take the essence of many of their themes and combine them into a prayer. As the outcome is long, I have split the prayer into 'stanzas' so that you can mediate on one each day and then pray through it afterwards.

Let's start with thanksgiving.

Thank you for forming my heart,
Thank you for capturing my heart,
Thank you for sending the Spirit of your Son into my heart,
Thank you that you dwell in my heart,
Thank you that your word is in my heart,
Thank you that you alone know my heart,

Thank you that your heart yearns for me, for my heart.

Now Search Out the Matter
---

1. Write a poem or a letter to God expressing your love for Him and thanking Him for His love for you.

2. What will you do to place even more of His word in your heart?

3. Have you allowed Holy Spirit into every room in your heart? Are some locked?

MY HEART'S STATE

My heart is full of reverence for you,
My heart is stirred by a noble theme,
My heart rejoices in your salvation,
My heart will sing praises to you,
My heart will not be silent,
My heart trusts in you,
My heart is set on a pilgrimage,
My heart burns when you talk with me,
My heart is broken and contrite,
My heart cries out to you, the living God

Now Search Out the Matter

---

1. Describe the current state of your heart in written form, using the kind of structure above. Be honest with yourself!

2. Is the current state of your heart anywhere close to that which is described above? If not, what needs to change?

3. What would it look like for your heart to be 'set on a pilgrimage?

A PRAYER FOR MY HEART

Grant me an undivided heart,
Grant me a wise heart,
Grant me a wise heart to know the proper time,
Grant me a secure heart without fear,
Grant me the heart of a lion,
Grant me a discerning heart,
Grant me a cheerful heart as a continual feast,
Grant me singleness of heart and action,
Grant me a heart of flesh,
Grant me a gentle heart,
Grant me a glad and sincere heart,
Grant me a heart of gratitude,
Grant me to be a person after your heart,
Grant me a responsive and humble heart.

Now Search Out the Matter

---

1. What would your heart look like if it was undivided?

2. What would have to change for your heart to be as 'cheerful as a continual feast?

3. How many of the Kings in the Old Testament were said to have fully devoted their hearts to the Lord like David?

PRAY THIS THIS FOR YOUR HEART

Fill my heart with joy,
Soak my heart in peace,
Banish anxiety from my heart,
Relieve the troubles of my heart,
Fill my heart with your wisdom,
Move my heart with love for you and for others,
Place plans in my heart to accomplish your purposes.

Heal the anguish of my heart,
Let your fire burn within my heart,
Fulfil my heart's desires,
Make my heart a stream of waters in your hand,
Move my heart to give,
Instruct my heart.

Strengthen my heart with grace,
Guard my heart,
Search, probe, weigh and test my heart,
Carry me close to your heart,
Calm my disturbed heart.
Purify my heart,
Revive my heart.

Open my heart to your words,
Pour your love into my heart,
Make your light shine in my heart,
Enlighten my heart
Encourage my heart,
Direct my heart,
Refresh my heart.

Now Search Out the Matter

1. Pray the above prayer every day for a week and listen to Holy Spirit as he indicates any lines that resonate with your heart's desire.

2. Now pray over these one by one each day for the following week.

3. Write down a practical step you will take, partnering with Holy Spirit, for each of those heart desires.

MY HEART'S RESPONSE

I will seek you with all my heart,
I will love you with all my heart,
I will obey you with all my heart,
I will serve you with all my heart,
I will turn to you with all my heart,
I will walk faithfully before you with all my heart,
I will follow you with all my heart,
I will extol you with all my heart,
I will trust you with all my heart.
I will devote my heart to you,
I will incline my heart to fear you,
I will yield my heart to you,
I will maintain an upright heart,
I will commit my whole heart to you,
I will speak truth from my heart,
I will remain steadfast of heart,
I will pour my heart out to you, hear my cry,
I will apply my heart to understanding,
I will forgive others from my heart,
I will write love and faithfulness on the tablet of my heart,
I will set my heart on the right path,
I will not set my heart on riches,
I will make music to you from my heart,
I will not forget your goodness or let it fade from my heart,
I will be one in heart with all my brothers and sisters,
I will not lose heart when you rebuke me,

The purposes of my heart are deep waters,
And my life reflects my heart,
I give you my heart -
Thank you for setting eternity in my heart!

May the meditation of my heart be pleasing in your sight!

Now Search Out the Matter

1. Pray the above prayer, but don't rush. Consider each line of surrender before you pray it. If you are not ready to pray that line, then move to the next one.

2. What action will you take in response to one or more lines in this prayer?

3. Is everything you think (meditate) about in your heart pleasing in God's sight?

HOLY SPIRIT

- ❖ Equipped For Victory
- ❖ Alongside
- ❖ Paraklesis
- ❖ Watermark
- ❖ Thirsty
- ❖ Refreshment
- ❖ Waymaker

'The Holy Spirit is in me for my sake, but upon me for yours.'

'Much of today's church relies more on a book the early church didn't have, than the Holy Spirit they did'

Bill Johnson

EQUIPPED FOR VICTORY

It is true that you sometimes stand in front of the impossible, however,
you also stand in my presence, in front of the Almighty.
Who do you think will prevail?

At times you may want to move forward,
to discover new things.
Take your time.
It is better to find richness in one thing,
than to rush into much without thought.
I have the schedule worked out -
you don't need to find a more efficient way!
Read my word, listen to me, keep looking up
and all will be made clear.
You have much to learn.
Keep your heart open.
My Kingdom is your priority.

Surprises may lie ahead,
but I will equip you with everything that you need.
Grace will overflow.
It will more than match each challenge.
The battle may be tough, but you will come through victorious.
You share my honour, my power, and my authority.
You are a child of the king.
Never doubt your standing,
take hold of all that has been made available to you.
You will not walk alone.
Be strong.
Avail yourself of my armour.
Victory lies ahead because victory has long been secured!

Now Search Out the Matter

1. How have you been equipped for victory? What has been made available to you?

2. Search out three Old Testament stories where victory was achieved. How did this come about? How can you translate what you have learned and apply it in your life?

3. Is victory ever a result of what you do?

ALONGSIDE

My first full time job was in a Telecommunications company who sent half a dozen of its new starters on a series of six excellent leadership courses. I was delighted to be included. Back in the 70's and 80's, Outward Bound courses were very much in vogue for leadership training in the UK, and it was no surprise that one of our six development courses adopted this training vehicle.

One afternoon exercise placed us at the foot of a rock face which was 15-20 metre high, and we were told that we would need to climb to the top and then abseil back down. I had grown to love walking and scrambling in the hills and mountains, but I had never climbed. I never even succeeded in climbing a vertical rope in our school gym - I had, and have, no great strength in my arms.

This climb was presented to us rated as a 'V Diff', simply meaning 'Very Difficult'. This is a slightly misleading term, as there are many more demanding grades of climb above this in the rankings! Nevertheless, this seemed quite a daunting challenge for a beginner! Inevitably, I was both excited and very nervous.

Some who went before me reached the top relatively quickly. Others struggled, but still made it all the way. Then my turn came. I made steady progress to begin with, if a little slow. About halfway up, my right boot slipped off the narrow rock edge it had been on as I attempted to move myself upwards and to reach for the next handhold. Thus far, I had climbed with my whole body hugging the rock. I was to learn that, whilst this seems a safer approach, it yields less leverage for both your hands and feet than if you keep your main torso away from the rock face.

I tried to hold on tightly, but with the sudden loss of one foothold, I started to slide under the law of gravity, losing my grip on the wet rock and taking some skin off my fingers as I slipped downwards whilst desperately trying to hold on.

I was fully roped up, and I didn't descend very far at all, as the trainer at the top held the rope, and thus me, securely. My heart was beating faster with the suddenness of my slip. My pride was dented, knowing all my peers were looking on. I froze. I was once again, clinging as closely as I could to the rock face, breathing rapidly. I looked up helplessly at how I would re-ascend the short distance that I had dropped, let alone complete the climb.

That was the moment I will never forget. As I held on wondering what to do next, I noticed a figure above me. An expert climber was climbing downwards from the top with ease, and without a rope! (Something you should never do). He was the nearest thing to Spiderman that I have ever seen! He climbed on down until he was parallel to me on my right.

What followed surprised me. He didn't orchestrate me being lowered back to the ground using the rope, nor did he move across and support me up to the next handhold. He simply, and very calmly, coached me. He told me, one by one, which holds to take, and he climbed in sync with me so I could always see him at my side a few metres away. As a result, I was at the top in no time, and under my own steam, albeit with his expert guidance. That did a lot to reinstate my self-belief and spurred me on to tackle my first abseil which followed shortly after my ascent. I had been much more anxious about the abseil than the climb! I now knew for sure that I could trust both the rope and my teachers. I enjoyed the thrill of abseiling down and was even disappointed that the latter experience passed so quickly!

THE GLORY OF KINGS

I have often looked back on this climb and whilst praying for a couple of pastors in Sweden God brought this memory back. What follows is what the Father seemed to be saying to me as I reflected on the parallels between that event and how He has placed Holy Spirit alongside us as we walk with Him.

A word from your Father...

My child,

Where you find yourself may seem 'very difficult'
and you may get stuck along the way.
Going backwards is not the way forward!
I need you to hold on just where you are and
remember, I will always be alongside.

There are times when I will remove obstacles.
There are times when you will attain new heights.
I've designed you to be an overcomer, to breakthrough.
You may experience fear, pain, and humiliation.
But remember, I am always alongside.

I never said the climb was easy.
I equipped you before you set out.
The rope you are holding onto is secure.
Just cry out to me for help
and you'll sense me alongside.

Listen carefully and I'll show you where to place your feet.
I'll point to where your hands will be secure.
I know the route you're taking,
because I took it before you.
And now I'm here, right by your side!

Always alongside!

Now Search Out the Matter

1. Spend time giving thanks that Holy Spirit always dwells in you, is always alongside you and longs to rest on you.

2. What spiritual rock face do you need to climb or to overcome? Now acknowledge His presence and hold on tight as you listen to His guidance. The tougher the issue, the more that Holy Spirit has to offer you. His help is never lacking, forever relevant, and always available.

3. What are you clinging on to, instead of resting free?

PARAKLESIS

The Greek word paraklésis (παράκλησις) means to 'come alongside'. Its use in the New Testament can indicate encouragement, comfort, exhortation, appeal, consolation, urgency and preaching.

The word paraklétos shares the same Greek root and means one who advocates for another, helper, comforter, intercessor, strengthener, standby. The word is used by John four times in his gospel (John 14:16-17, 26; John15:26 and John 16:7). Jesus promises to ask the Father to give the disciples...

> "...another advocate to help you and be with you for ever – the Spirit of truth. The world cannot accept him, because it neither sees him nor knows him. But you know him, for he lives with you and will be in you."

> "But the Advocate, the Holy Spirit, whom the Father will send in my name, will teach you all things and will remind you of everything I have said to you."

The word Paraklete is most often used to refer to the Holy Spirit. However, the word is also used to describe Jesus as 'advocate' in 1 John 2:1

> 'We have an advocate with the Father – Jesus Christ, the Righteous One.'

And in 2 Corinthians 1:3 we see the word Paraklesos (comfort) used to describe the Father:

> 'Praise be to the God and Father of our Lord Jesus Christ, the Father of compassion and the God of all comfort.'

Whilst the word is typically understood by us today to refer to the Holy Spirit, it is no surprise that it is a characteristic of all persons in the Godhead!

Interestingly, the purpose of prophecy is provided by Paul in 1 Corinthians 14:3 and is one way that God comes alongside us through others in the body of Christ:

> 'But the one who prophesies speaks to people for their strengthening, encouraging and comfort.'

Here the Greek words are: -

Strengthening – oikodomé (οἰκοδομή) building up, edifying
Encouraging – paraklésis (παράκλησις) encouragement
Comfort – paramuthia (παραμυθία) exhortation, comfort

The Godhead living in us wants to strengthen, encourage and comfort us, and then flow through us to others so that they are strengthened, encouraged and comforted!

This is so well expressed by Paul in 2 Corinthians 1:3-5 (MSG)

> 'All praise to the God and Father of our Master, Jesus the Messiah! Father of all mercy! God of all healing counsel! He comes alongside us when we go through hard times, and before you know it, he brings us alongside someone else who is going through hard times so that we can be there for that person just as God was there for us. We have plenty of hard times that come from following the Messiah, but no more so than the good times of his healing comfort—we get a full measure of that, too.'

Now Search Out the Matter

1. Reflect on the times in recent months when Holy Spirit came alongside you and built you up, or encouraged you, or comforted you. Write these down, and then spend time in thanksgiving and worship.

2. Think about some of the tough seasons that you have faced and come through with the Holy Spirit's help. Read 2 Corinthians 1:3-5 in a range of different Bible versions. How can you take what you learned from those hard times and from how Holy Spirit came alongside you and now use it to help others?

3. Who do you know who needs building up, encouraging, exhorting or comforting? Select 2 or 3 people, note down their names and the way in which you are going to make this a reality for each of them by partnering with Holy Spirit.

4. Pray for them right now!

WATERMARK

Banknotes made from paper were introduced by the Bank of England in 1694. It was the debut of the world's first national currency. In 1695 the first counterfeit notes were produced driving the Bank to figure out ways to secure the genuine currency. In 1697 manufactured watermarked paper was produced on smaller denomination banknotes. Watermarks are designs or images embedded into the paper during the manufacturing process to add security, and they can be seen when the banknote is held up to the light.

English banknotes also carry an inscription: 'I promise to pay the bearer on demand the sum of five pounds' (or ten, twenty, fifty according to the value of the note). The watermark provides authenticity to the owner of the banknote and the inscription carries the promise of its value. These watermarks were used for over 300 years until new polymer notes were introduced in 2016, and the inscriptions still appear on the current banknotes!

The concept of the Holy Spirit as a seal of salvation is found in several passages in the Bible. Here are some of the key references:

'And you also were included in Christ when you heard the message of truth, the gospel of your salvation. When you believed, you were marked in him with a seal, the promised Holy Spirit, who is a deposit guaranteeing our inheritance until the redemption of those who are God's possession – to the praise of his glory.'

Ephesians 1:13-14

'Now it is God who makes both us and you stand firm in Christ. He anointed us, set his seal of ownership on us, and put his Spirit in our hearts as a deposit, guaranteeing what is to come.'

2 Corinthians 1:21-22

'And do not grieve the Holy Spirit of God, with whom you were sealed for the day of redemption.'
Ephesians 4:30

These passages emphasize the Holy Spirit as a seal, a guarantee, and an indication of God's ownership and protection of believers. The Holy Spirit is thus just like a watermark on the believer – a sign of authenticity that we are children of God.

The Holy Spirit is frequently symbolised by water throughout scripture, and having a bit of fun with words now, He is God's 'Water-Mark' on us, a 'Holy Spirit-Mark' on us!

Watermarks on banknotes are indelible – just as the Holy Spirit's mark on us is indelible. The term 'indelible' is defined as:-

> 'A mark that cannot be removed;
> a mark which is impossible to eliminate, erase, or forget; one which is lasting and permanent
> and leaves an enduring impression or impact.'

Holy Spirit is our 'watermark' and cannot be eliminated, erased, forgotten and who is lasting, enduring and permanent!

Furthermore, the Holy Spirit is also like the bank note inscription. He is 'a deposit guaranteeing our inheritance' to us as bearers – we carry him from the moment of our salvation right through to eternal life!!! He personifies an inscription promising eternal value to us, as well as an assurance that all God's promises in Christ to us are 'yes and amen':

> 'For no matter how many promises God has made, they are 'Yes' in Christ. And so through him the 'Amen' is spoken by us to the glory of God.'
>
> 2 Corinthians 1:20

Now Search Out the Matter

---

1. How valuable are you to God? Think of as many proofs as you can that underwrite your value to Him and write them down. Note how certain they each are.

2. Take one of the promises which God has given you and pray this, "Lord you promised to pay (fulfil) this sum (your word) to me (the bearer) on demand (His promise to you)"

THIRSTY

This is a story of a hike that I undertook 40 years ago, and which God brought back to mind recently.

It took place in Derbyshire and was a 'challenge walk' known then as the 'High Peak Marathon'. I recall it being 40 miles long to be covered within one day. It involved over 7,000 feet of ascent and descent during the day. But in reality the walk was even more demanding.

When I planned the walk using a map of the area and route, I had no clue that, what appeared to be a level easy walking, section from West to East would turn out to be much more of an obstacle course in every sense! That area was aptly called (I learned the hard way!) 'Bleaklow'.

It is a high up gritstone moorland covered in boggy peat seamed by 'groughs' (pronounced 'gruffs'). These are channels which have been eroded by water in the peat and wind tortuously across most of the plateau. They are disconnected and cut into the landscape at every possible angle, in a seemingly random fashion. Typically, they are 2-3 metres deep, and to cross each one you must slide down one side and take a run at the far side to climb out. The peat is spongy, and with water added, the tread on the soles of your boots soon clogs up with peat. Your boots lose all their grip causing you to slide back down to the bottom and then have to take a second run-up! A few groughs kindly ran in the direction of travel, but many ran across it! And to add to the fun, once in the bottom of a grough you lose all sense of direction. When you climb out, you find very few landmarks to aid your traverse of the moorland.

Even in bright sunshine of that July day, these groughs became frustrating and exhausting, and they put us well behind our planned schedule. Their repetitive descent and ascent were at least as wearisome as climbing much higher mountains. (In case any of you are put off from making this hike, the rest of it is simply glorious and well worth the effort!)

We had started out that day with full bottles of water, but it was a scorching July day – and clear enough for us to get a suntan! Our water ran out before we were halfway around. We were able to refill our bottles at Kinder Downfall but by the time we had traversed Bleaklow, we were out of water again with some 30% of the course still to go. I have **never** been so thirsty!! Worse still, we only had a little cash with us, and when we finally got back to where the car was parked, we only had sufficient cash to buy and share one drink!

Jesus answered, 'Everyone who drinks this water will be thirsty again, but whoever drinks the water I give them will never thirst. Indeed, the water I give them will become in them a spring of water welling up to eternal life." John 4:13-14

'On the last and greatest day of the festival, Jesus stood and said in a loud voice, 'Let anyone who is thirsty come to me and drink. Whoever believes in me, as Scripture has said, rivers of living water will flow from within them." John 7:37-38

Now Search Out the Matter

1. Can you say with the Psalmist…?

   'As the deer pants for streams of water, so my soul pants for you, my God. My soul thirsts for God, for the living God. When can I go and meet with God?'

   Psalm 42:1-2

   'You, God, are my God, earnestly I seek you; I thirst for you, my whole being longs for you, in a dry and parched land where there is no water.'

   Psalm 63:1

2. How **thirsty** are you for more of Holy Spirit? Are you **desperate** for a drink?

3. Have you faced many barren and difficult ups-and-downs in life and come through exhausted and thirsty?

REFRESHMENT

I made a second hike during another summer in the area surrounding Ben Nevis. Earlier in the week I had climbed the Ben via a tricky but thrilling route with stunning views. It had been a long walk in (and back) to the 'Bed & Breakfast' where I was staying.

A few days later I took on a less strenuous but still demanding walk. I had sufficient water, but the ascent from Kinlochleven over the high tops and down into Glen Nevis was draining. It was the hottest summer in the West of Scotland for 40 years, and that day had a lot of cloud cover, making the going tough with extremely humid conditions. I was covered in perspiration and probably not someone to be standing next to! The mosquitos were my unwelcome friends!

Having scaled the high point, I then descended into Glen Nevis. After some time, now walking in the shade of trees and away from the heat of the sun, I came across a waterfall, perhaps 5-6 metres high with a small, but deep, pool at its foot. The pool was surrounded by a cliff face on two sides. It wasn't a tough decision to strip off and dive in, immersing myself in the beautiful cold and pure mountain water. To this day, I still recall the instant refreshment that this brought. I thoroughly enjoyed the moment swimming, or just treading water, before continuing my hike. It was a transforming time. I emerged from the water feeling clean and completely revived.

Now Search Out the Matter

1. How much do you need complete **refreshment?** Is it time to go beyond just dipping your toe into the water? Is it time for full **immersion** in the Holy Spirit?

   'I will refresh the weary and satisfy the faint.'
   Jeremiah 31:25

2. Has it ever occurred to you that you are made in the image of a God who rested and was refreshed? If He needed rest, how much more do you!!!!

   'It will be a sign between me and the Israelites for ever, for in six days the LORD made the heavens and the earth, and on the seventh day he rested and was refreshed.'
   Exodus 31:17

3. Maybe you are okay as you read this, your thirst quenched. Wonderful! But there's more!! And maybe you need to refresh others now. In giving you receive! Who needs your refreshment?

   'A generous person will prosper;
   whoever refreshes others will be refreshed.'
   Proverbs 11:25

WAYMAKER

I am the Way the Truth and the Life.
No-one comes to the Father but by me.
I am the door.
Open the door when you hear my knock.
Open the door when you hear my voice.

Acknowledge me and I will make your paths straight.
I've gone into your future and cleared the way.
I have removed all the obstacles.
I've made the path smooth.
I've set your feet on rock.
I've steadied your footsteps.
I've established your path.

I know where you are destined.
I see and guide your every step.
My word is a lamp to your feet and
a light to your path.
I gently draw you back when you wander off.
I do not scold you, but love you back onto the right path,
in the right direction.

Will you walk with me to Emmaus?
Will you let me unfold the Scriptures to you?
Will you break bread with me and gives thanks?

Will you listen out for my Spirit's softly spoken guidance?
Will you trust me to direct you?
Will you walk in obedience to my commands?
Will you remain steadfast and full of faith when the going gets tough?

You do not walk alone.
You'll never walk alone!
Nothing can separate you from my love.
Nothing.

Now Search Out the Matter

---

1. Re-read the seven 'Will you' statements above and tell Holy Spirit if you are willing.

2. Review the following texts and make a note of what they teach about 'the way-maker': John 14:6; Psalm 139; Psalm 119:105; Revelation 3:20; Proverbs 3:5-6; Psalm 40:1-5; Romans 8:31-39.

3. What step do you need to take to allow Him to make a way for you based on Proverbs 3:6? Now invite Holy Spirit into an area where you need breakthrough.

RELATIONSHIP

- ❖ Be To Them As I Am To You
- ❖ One Another
- ❖ All Or Some
- ❖ Personalize
- ❖ Never
- ❖ Ever And Ever
- ❖ Keep In The Blessing

*'Four of the Ten Commandments deal with
our relationship with God
while the other six deal with our
relationships with people.
But all ten are about relationships.'*

Rick Warren

BE TO THEM AS I AM TO YOU

In your weakness, I give you strength.
Introduce my strength to the weak.

In your disappointment, I encourage you.
Carry my encouragement to those who are striving.

In your suffering, I comfort you.
Pour out my comfort on the distressed.

In your grief, I console you.
Share my consolation with those overwhelmed by grief.

In your feebleness, I help you.
Support your brothers and sisters in their struggles.

In your loneliness, I come alongside you.
Embrace the lonely with your time and love.

In your failure, I exhort you.
In my love, plead with those who have strayed.

In your challenges, I intercede for you.
Pray for those you love and refresh them with kindness.

In your stumbling, I exhort you to come higher.
Cheer on all who are stuck - urge them forwards.

In your hunger and thirst, I give you manna and water,
Feed my sheep.

Now Search Out the Matter

1. Ask Holy Spirit to show you two people who need your help and use the above to inform yourself of what you need to do.

2. Prayerfully figure out the best way to show your love for these individuals and make your plan to support them a reality this week. Now pray for them.

3. Pray for the opportunity to implement your plans. In some cases, you won't need to wait and 'take' an opportunity provided to you – instead, you might simply need to be proactive in 'making' that opportunity. Call someone, invite them over for a coffee, pray with them, message them, take them a gift, send them a card, etc.

   A one-off action of kindness can be a real boost to another. However, a sustained demonstration of kindness is likely to have a much greater and long-lasting impact - but comes at a higher personal cost.

ONE ANOTHER

Love *one another*
Accept *one another*
Forgive *one another*
Instruct *one another*
Bear with *one another*
Submit to *one another*
Encourage *one another*
Agree with *one another*
Be devoted to *one another*
Humbly serve *one another*
Offer hospitality to *one another*
Have fellowship with *one another*
Live in harmony with *one another*
With a holy kiss, greet *one another*
Be patient, bearing with *one another*
With wisdom, admonish *one another*
Honour, above yourselves, *one another*
Stop passing judgement on *one another*
Be kind and compassionate to *one another*
With love and good deeds, spur on *one another*
Have the same mindset as Jesus with *one another*
Clothe yourselves with humility toward *one another*
Speak psalms, hymns, songs from the spirit to *one another*

Now Search Out the Matter

1. Select three of the 'one another' expectations found in God's Word. Don't just pick those in which you are already operating – if you want to grow in love and in serving the body of Christ, then you need to stretch yourself!

2. Now spend time in prayer and ask Holy Spirit to direct you to the people whom you need to love in a new way, at least one person for each for the areas you selected above.

3. Now write down a plan of how and when you are going to activate this new avenue of blessing to those around you.

4. Once you've blessed some people, write down what happened, what the impact was on them (and you) and give thanks that you have these opportunities every day.

ALL OR SOME?

Which is the closest description of how you think and live?

And we know that **some** things work together for good to them that love God, to them who are the called according to his purpose. Your Life Version???	**OR**	**Romans 8:28** And we know that **all** things work together for good to them that love God, to them who are the called according to his purpose. King James Version
Some scripture is inspired by God and profitable for teaching, for reproof, for correction, and for training in righteousness. Your Life Version???	**OR**	**2 Timothy 3:16** **All** scripture is inspired by God and profitable for teaching, for reproof, for correction, and for training in righteousness. Revised Standard Version
But seek first his kingdom and his righteousness, and **some** of these things will be given to you as well. Your Life Version???	**OR**	**Matthew 6:33** But seek first his kingdom and his righteousness, and **all** these things will be given to you as well. New International Version

---

Now Search Out the Matter

It can be easy to read the truth in the Word and mentally acknowledge it. It's a different thing to allow it to change how we think and act. Sometimes we are not even aware of the misalignment between what we think and what the truth is in Christ and how we are currently living it out.

1. Romans 8:28 doesn't say that 'all things **are** good', nor does it say that '**some** things work together for good'. Think of a recent life event that set you back and check if you can confidently say 'I know that all things work together for good…' in your life.

2. Can you give 'thanks **in** all circumstances' in line with 1 Thessalonians 5:16-18? It doesn't say '**for** all circumstances!'. Get the difference between 'in' and 'for' sorted out in your head! What circumstance do you need to give thanks in, despite it being painful, or irritating, or hard to understand?

3. Read Matthew 6:19-34. Are you worried about food, clothing or money? Are there any areas of your life where you are seeking something else as a higher priority than the Kingdom? (Career, status, money, relationships, fun, etc). If you are not sure, consider how you spent your time in the last week.

PERSONALIZE

There are several simple approaches to acquiring a new perspective as you read and meditate on the Bible. Here is one example...

Make an appropriate word switch and read the passage out loud. Try it now with 1 Corinthians 13:4-7. Replace each occurrence of the word 'love' with 'I' as you read. You may have to substitute a few other words to make sense. To get you started, I'll put the original and personalized text below:

New International Version	Personalized Version
Love is patient, love is kind. It does not envy, it does not boast, it is not proud. It does not dishonour others, it is not self-seeking, it is not easily angered, it keeps no record of wrongs. Love does not delight in evil but rejoices with the truth. It always protects, always trusts, always hopes, always perseveres.	I am patient, I am kind. I do not envy, I do not boast, I am not proud. I do not dishonour others, I am not self-seeking, I am not easily angered, I keep no record of wrongs. I do not delight in evil but rejoice with the truth. I always protect, I always trust, I always hope, I always persevere.

How do you measure up?

Now try it again, and this time replace the word 'Love' by 'Jesus' instead.
Any new thoughts?

Now try this. Take Ephesians 1:13-14 and replace 'you' with 'I' and 'our' and 'your' with 'my':

New International Version	Personalized Version
And you also were included in Christ when you heard the message of truth, the gospel of your salvation. When you believed, you were marked in him with a seal, the promised Holy Spirit, who is a deposit guaranteeing our inheritance until the redemption of those who are God's possession—to the praise of his glory.	And I also was included in Christ when I heard the message of truth, the gospel of my salvation. When I believed, I was marked in him with a seal, the promised Holy Spirit, who is a deposit guaranteeing my inheritance until the redemption of those who are God's possession—to the praise of his glory.

Now Search Out the Matter

Got the idea? OK, experiment with these passages and see if personalizing them influences how you perceive your standing in Christ, or how you behave, or how you might need to change.

- Psalm 91:3-16 (replace you by 'I' or 'me' and 'your' by 'my'
- 2 Corinthians 1:3-4 (replace 'us' by 'me' and 'we' by 'I')
- 2 Peter 1:3-4 (replace 'us' by 'me' and 'you' by 'I')
- Titus 3:5-7 (replace 'us' by 'me' and 'you' by 'I')
- Hebrews 4:15-16 (replace 'us' by 'me' and 'you' by 'I')
- Ephesians 6:14-18 (switch 'you' to 'I', 'your' to 'my' and insert 'I will' before 'stand', 'take', 'pray' and 'be alert')

NEVER

His compassions	*never*	fail
His kingdom is one that will	*never*	be destroyed
His kingdom will	*never*	end
His righteousness will	*never*	fail
His words will	*never*	pass away
Whoever comes to me will	*never*	go hungry
Whoever comes to me I will	*never*	drive away
Whoever follows me will	*never*	walk in darkness
Whoever obeys my word will	*never*	see death
Whoever lives by believing in me will	*never*	die
Whoever drinks the water I give them will	*never*	thirst
He will	*never*	leave you or forsake you
I will	*never*	break my covenant with you
God will	*never*	forget the needy
He will	*never*	let the righteous be shaken
He will	*never*	forsake his inheritance
Blessed is the one whose sin the Lord will	*never*	count against them
The righteous will	*never*	be shaken
The righteous will	*never*	be uprooted
You will	*never*	be put to shame or disgraced
You will be like a spring whose waters	*never*	fail
May I	*never*	boast except in the cross of our Lord Jesus Christ
Love	*never*	fails

Now Search Out the Matter

1. Read the 'Never' list of promises. Are there any lies you are believing where the way in which you behave, or think would indicate a mindset of 'sometimes' within these verses? For example: 'Love sometimes fails' or 'He who comes to me will sometimes go hungry' and so on.

2. Pick 5 of these 'Never' promises. Find the verses where these promises are made and then write them on a card. Keep this card in your wallet, or in your handbag, or stick it in a prominent place on a wall and then declare them out loud every day for a month.

3. How will you use some of these truths to encourage those with whom you share fellowship?

EVER AND EVER

This God is our God for *ever and ever*

Your throne, O God, will last for *ever and ever*

To him be the power for *ever and ever*

He will reign for *ever and ever*

To our God and Father be glory for *ever and ever*

To him be glory in the church and in Christ Jesus throughout all generations, for *ever and ever*

I am the Living One; I was dead, and now look, I am alive for *ever and ever*

All the nations may walk in the name of their gods, but we will walk in the name of the Lord our God for *ever and ever*

Those who are wise will shine like the brightness of the heavens, and those who lead many to righteousness, like the stars for *ever and ever*

But the holy people of the Most High will receive the kingdom and will possess it for *ever and ever*

To the King eternal, immortal, invisible, the only God, be honour and glory for *ever and ever*

Praise and glory and wisdom and thanks and honour and power and strength be to our God for *ever and ever*

I trust in God's unfailing love for *ever and ever*

I will always obey your law, for *ever and ever*

I will exalt you, my God the King; I will praise your name for *ever and ever*

Every day I will praise you and extol your name for *ever and ever*

Let every creature praise his holy name for *ever and ever*

Now Search Out the Matter

1. Write a summary paragraph (as short as you can!) that covers the first 10 of these 'forever and ever' truths.

2. What are the implications of all these 'forever and ever' truths for you? If you fully believed all of them, what difference would it make to the way you live and worship?

3. Now write a personal prayer which is constructed around the last seven 'forever and ever' statements and use it each morning this week.

KEEP IN THE BLESSING

During the season where COVID was rife 'The Blessing' song was released by Cody Carnes, Kari Jobe and Elevation Worship. Like COVID, it also went viral around the world, with lyrics based on several scriptures: Numbers 6:22-27, Exodus 20:6 and Exodus 33:14. I was really blessed by it during that difficult time! As I was singing along to it a while ago, it struck me that I wasn't completely sure what the word 'keep' meant in – 'The Lord keep you'. Things I keep are in boxes, drawers, shelves, the loft, sheds and my mind - but this clearly wasn't the meaning in Hebrew! The Hebrew word for 'keep' is shamar (שָׁמַר) – but what does that mean? I decided to dig deeper by looking at where else this word was used in the Old Testament.

'For he will command his angels concerning you to **guard** you in all your ways.' Psalm 91:11

'David replied, 'No, my brothers, you must not do that with what the Lord has given us. He has **protected** us and delivered into our hands the raiding party that came against us.' 1 Samuel 30:23

Hannah's prayer in 1 Samuel 2:9 'He will **guard** the feet of his faithful servants.'

Job 29:2 'How I long for the months gone by, for the days when God **watched over me**.'

Psalm 16:1 '**Keep me safe**, my God, for in you I take refuge.'

Genesis 28:15 'I am with you and will **watch over** you wherever you go, and I will bring you back to this land. I will not leave you until I have done what I have promised you.'

Exodus 23:20 'See, I am sending an angel ahead of you **to guard you** along the way and to bring you to the place I have prepared.'

Joshua 24:17 'He **protected us** on our entire journey and among all the nations through which we travelled.'

Psalm 121:3-5 'He will not let your foot slip – **he who watches over you** will not slumber; indeed, he who watches over Israel will neither slumber nor sleep. The Lord **watches over you** – the Lord is your shade at your right hand.'

Psalms 121:7-8 'The Lord will keep you from all harm – **he will watch over** your life; the Lord **will watch over** your coming and going both now and for evermore.'

'for the Lord will be at your side and **will keep** your foot from being snared.' Proverbs 3:26

Psalm 127:1 'Unless the Lord builds the house, the builders labour in vain. Unless the Lord **watches over** the city, the **guards** stand watch in vain.'

I then decided to write my own kind of 'Amplified Version' using the Brown-Driver-Briggs definition and the prior passages and their context:

The Lord Bless you and *sustain you.*
The Lord Bless you and *preserve you.*
The Lord Bless you and *guard you in all your ways.*
The Lord *keep you from all harm.*
The Lord Bless you and *protect and deliver you.*
The Lord Bless and *guard your feet so that you do not stumble.*
The Lord Bless you and *watch over your life and wherever you go.*
The Lord Bless you and *keep you safe.*
The Lord Bless you and *protect you always and everywhere.*
The Lord Bless you and *guard the way ahead with angels.*

> The Lord *bring you to the place He has prepared.*
>
> The Lord who Blesses you,
> and watches over you,
> **Never** lets your foot slip!
> and **Never** sleeps!
>
> the Lord make his face shine on you
> and be gracious to you;
> the Lord turn his face towards you
> and give you peace.

Leaving the other parts of the Aaronic Blessing to one side, I was even more intrigued by the verse which follows it, found in Numbers 6:27. Have you ever noticed this?

'So they will put my name on the Israelites, and I will bless them.'

Aaron and his sons were to bless the Israelites, and each time they did, God would 'put His name on them and bless them'!

Now Search Out the Matter
---

1. What was being implied here in the phrase 'so they will put my name on them'? (Numbers 6:27). What does it mean that He puts His name on us today?

2. What do the words 'The Lord make His face shine on you' (Numbers 6:25) mean to you?

3. Look at the following verses and see if you can expand this line in the same way as above. Look in each verse below, select the phrase (or context) that uses the same Hebrew word and create an expanded prayer version e.g. using Psalm 80:7,19 we could say 'The Lord make His face shine on you that you may be saved'. Now add lines from these verses or contexts:
    a. Exodus 25:37
    b. Isaiah 60:19
    c. Psalm 80:7
    d. Psalm 77:18
    e. Psalm 19:8
    f. Psalm 119:130
    g. Psalm 119:135

4. What does this mean to you 'The Lord turn His face towards you?'

GLORY

- ❖ Glory Manifest
- ❖ Glory Of The Lord
- ❖ Jesus' Glory
- ❖ The Nature Of Glory
- ❖ What His Glory Looks Like
- ❖ In Light Of His Glory
- ❖ The Glory Of Kings

*'It is the glory of God
to conceal a matter;
to search out a matter
is the glory of kings'*

Proverbs 25:2

GLORY MANIFEST

I've always been puzzled by exactly what glory means. When studying 2 Peter 1:3 (ESV), I decided to see what the Greek word was being used by Peter: it is 'doxa' (δόξα). According to Strong's Greek 1391, this word can be interpreted as 'honour, renown; glory, an especially divine quality, *the unspoken manifestation of God*, splendour.'

Fascinated by what the 'unspoken manifestation God might be, I determined to meditate on this. But first, I started with the easier, more obvious counterpart:

The spoken manifestation of God

Jesus
His Word
Creation

His revelation through us via
Prophecy
Words of knowledge
Words of wisdom
Preaching
Teaching

Our
Worship
Praise
Thanksgiving
Testimony

I then turned my thoughts to the 'unspoken manifestation of God'. I may have missed some, but here's my list:

The unspoken manifestation of God

His omnipresence
His Holy Spirit
His splendour
His majesty
His light
His sovereignty
His holiness
His purity
His beauty
His omnipotence
His divinity
His creation
His justice
His omniscience
His perfection
His grace
His immutability
His truth
His love
His peace
His eternity
His self-sufficiency
His wisdom
His power
His mercy
His kindness
His compassion
His worthiness
His mystery

Now Search Out the Matter

1. Review these two lists (the spoken and unspoken manifestations of God) and add anything that you find is missing or make amendments if you disagree with my draft.

2. Read 2 Peter 1:1-15 (ESV), and then go back to verse 3. What do you think it means that He has 'called us to His own glory and excellence'. Consider the thoughts on glory above.

3. Read through the unspoken manifestations of God and pick one out which really strikes you. Ask Holy Spirit to reveal what God's glory looks like when He manifests this characteristic.

4. How should this change the way we think, behave and worship?

GLORY OF THE LORD

The next sections explore the topic of 'glory' in much more detail. I attempted to look at every reference where the word 'glory' appears throughout the Bible. I then grouped what I found under several different headings. This kind of study takes a long time but is rich in discovery. Review one section at a time and then dig deeper.

The Lord...

Is the King of glory
Reigns in glory
Is awesome in glory
Is clothed in glory, splendour, honour and majesty
Displays His glory
Is mysterious in His glory
Will not yield His glory to another

Now Search Out the Matter

---

1. We can sometimes steal God's glory – take it when in fact it was all due to Him. If you have, repent now and move on! Practice accrediting God with His glory daily.

2. What are the implications of His glory being mysterious?

JESUS' GLORY

Jesus...

Reveals His glory through miracles
Would not accept man's glory
Was glorified by His Father
Brought glory to His Father through obedience
Suffered before he entered into His glory
Sits on a glorious throne
Will come in His Father's power and great glory
Will return in His Father's, His own, and His angels' glory
Prayed to be returned to His Father's glory
Gives us the glory the Father gave Him so we would be one
Was raised from the dead through the glory of the Father
Has made the riches of God's glory known to us

Now Search Out the Matter

---

1. Do you accept man's glory?

2. Is there any act of obedience you haven't actioned which is withholding His glory?

3. What was Jesus' intention in giving us the glory that the Father gave Him? (John 17:22)

4. How was Jesus raised from the dead 'through the glory of the Father?'

THE GLORY OF KINGS

THE NATURE OF HIS GLORY

His Glory…

Surpasses earthly glory
Does not fade
Consecrates
Fills a place, a temple
Goes on filling a place
Fills the whole earth
Increases as His Kingdom grows
Was revealed in a burning bush
Thunders
Is eternal
Contains riches
Is the glory of His people
Was seen and spoken of by Isaiah
Came through those the Father gave Him
Was displayed in Jesus' face
Was displayed through the Gospel
Was glimpsed by His disciples
Was revealed through Lazarus' resurrection
Is alongside His power
Is found in His majesty
Crowns mankind
Is declared by the heavens
Shines through our victory
Dwells in His house
Opens the way for Him to enter
Is a shield around us
Is found in His name
Is due His name

THE GLORY OF KINGS

Is found in His sanctuary
Will be revered by kings
Is desired eternally
Is great
Moves and rises
Is memorable
Is given to those he chooses
Will be acknowledged vast and wide
Covers the heavens
Shines around angels

Now Search Out the Matter

---

1. How does His glory consecrate?

2. How are you living to increase His glory?

3. Who is given glory by God?

4. How was His glory revealed in a burning bush?

5. Does some of His glory come through us?

WHAT GLORY LOOKS LIKE

Glory May…

Appear, be seen and be revealed
Be given, gained, increased, and stripped from man
Look like a consuming fire
Be dangerous to man
Look like a dazzling light
Seem too dreadful to move into
Settle and cover
Not always be on show
Dwell in our land
Be likened to a rainbow and radiance
Will exceed our suffering now
Be turned into, or extinguished by shame

Now Search Out the Matter

---

1. How have you seen God's glory in your life?

2. In what sense do you understand His glory to be a 'consuming fire' or 'dangerous'?

3. Why do you think God's glory is not 'always on show'?

IN LIGHT OF HIS GLORY

We should...

Recognise that we have fallen short of His glory
Seek the glory of the Father
Contemplate His glory
Open the way for His glory to enter
Ascribe glory to God
Give Him the glory due His name
Give glory as part of our praise
Be led into worship by His glory
Sing glory to the Righteous One
Proclaim His glory
Fall face down in His glory
Live for the praise of His glory
Avoid seeking our own glory
Give glory to God by speaking the truth
Believe and we will see His glory forever
Not exchange God's glory for idols
Persist in doing good, seek glory and receive eternal life
Boast in the hope of the glory of God
Share in His suffering to share in His glory
Understand that we were prepared in advance for glory
Bring glory to God by standing on His promises
Gain glory by overlooking offences
Give Him glory through our unwavering faith
Live for the praise of His glory
Do everything for the glory of God

Now Search Out the Matter

Now contemplate His glory once again…

1. How do you 'seek the glory of the Father'?

2. How do you open the way 'for His glory to enter'?

3. How do you 'live for the 'praise of His glory'?

4. Have you 'shared in His glory' by 'sharing in His suffering'?

5. Are you aware that you are being 'prepared for His glory'? What does that look like in your life?

THE GLORY OF KINGS

> *'It is the glory of God to conceal a matter;*
> *to search out a matter is the glory of kings.'*
> Proverbs 25:2

The above verse is where the title of this book originated. I'd like you to take all that you have learned on this journey about 'searching out a matter' and try and figure out what this verse is all about. Without further ado, it's over to you now!

Now Search Out the Matter

---

1. How do you understand that 'it is the glory of God to conceal a matter?

2. What's the connection between God's glory and His right to conceal something?

3. What are the implications of this?

4. Why do you think 'searching out a matter' is the 'glory of kings'?

5. In what ways are the kings referred to here symbolic of all God's children?

6. Write your own paraphrase of this verse.

EPILOGUE

I pray that you have picked up a few new spiritual archaeological tools to dig deeper and carefully into God's Word. My dearest hope is that you have unearthed spiritual treasure as you have searched out many matters and that Holy Spirit has enriched your understanding of the character of God and His unmatched love.

If you have gone deeper and learned new things – don't stop now! Remember Jeremiah 29:13:

'You will seek me and find me when you seek me with all your heart.'

Whilst this book provides several different ways to investigate truth, there are undoubtedly more!

I would love to hear personal testimonies of how the Holy Spirit has used these devotions to inspire and enlighten you.

Please share your ideas, testimonies and the ways you hunt down the treasures in God's word:

phil.john@thegloryofkings.co.uk

Printed in Great Britain
by Amazon